Paula Vaughan
Romance WITH QUILTS

*P*aula Vaughan's pretty vignettes of a bygone
era – which often feature wonderfully detailed quilts –
have stirred our passion for these handmade treasures.
Reflecting her nostalgic images, this collection brings you ten
lovely quilts and fifteen decorative accessories to reproduce
for your own home. We used time-saving shortcuts and
contemporary methods that will allow you to create many of
these classic designs more quickly than quilters of yesteryear.
As you begin piecing these beautiful patterns, we hope that
Paula's soft country paintings and warm reminiscings
will nurture your own romance with quilts.

LEISURE ARTS, INC.
Little Rock, Arkansas

Jean Blanchard

Paula Vaughan
Romance WITH QUILTS

EDITORIAL STAFF

Vice President and Editor-in-Chief: Anne Van Wagner Childs
Executive Director: Sandra Graham Case
Design Director: Patricia Wallenfang Sowers
Editorial Director: Susan Frantz Wiles
Publications Director: Kristine Anderson Mertes
Creative Art Director: Gloria Bearden

TECHNICAL
Managing Editor: Sherry Solida Ford
Senior Technical Writer: Marley N. Washum
Technical Writers: Kimberly Smith and
    Barbara McClintock Vechik
Copy Editor: Susan Frazier
Production Assistant: Sharon Gillam

EDITORIAL
Managing Editor: Tammi Williamson Bradley
Associate Editor: Terri Leming Davidson

ART
Art Director: Rhonda Shelby
Senior Graphics Illustrator: Lora Prall-Puls
Graphics Illustrators: Rebecca Hester, John Rose,
    Dana Vaughn, and Wendy Willets
Color Technician: Mark Hawkins
Photography Stylists: Ellen J. Clifton, Tiffany Huffman,
    Elizabeth Lackey, and Janna Laughlin
Publishing Systems Administrator: Cynthia M. Lumpkin
Publishing Systems Assistant: Myra Means

PROMOTIONS
Managing Editor: Alan Caudle
Associate Editor: Steven M. Cooper
Designer: Dale Rowett
Art Director: Linda Lovette Smart

BUSINESS STAFF

Publisher: Rick Barton
Vice President and General Manager: Thomas L. Carlisle
Vice President, Finance: Tom Siebenmorgen
Director of Corporate Planning and Development:
    Laticia Mull Cornett.
Vice President, Retail Marketing: Bob Humphrey
Vice President, National Accounts: Pam Stebbins

Retail Marketing Director: Margaret Sweetin
General Merchandise Manager: Cathy Laird
Vice President, Operations: Jim Dittrich
Distribution Director: Rob Thieme
Retail Customer Service Manager: Wanda Price
Print Production Manager: Fred F. Pruss

International Standard Book Number 1-57486-182-4
10 9 8 7 6 5 4 3 2 1

INTRODUCING
PAULA VAUGHAN

*R*oses and romance and front porch swings — these are a few of Paula Vaughan's favorite things. It's no wonder her sentimental images of cherished antiques like quilts and pottery reflect the essence of a nostalgic era with such accuracy.

A woman of gentle spirit and generous lilting laughter, Paula is a beloved artist whose romantic images captured our hearts and imaginations. As evidenced by her painting, Paula holds a particular fondness for the artistry of needlewomen — the seamstress, the embroiderer, and especially the quilter.

"I've always felt that quilts were the way country women expressed themselves."

Her love of needlework goes back as far as she can remember. When Paula was young, her mother and grandmothers introduced her to the expressive possibilities of this medium. "I began each summer with a host of embroidery projects," she recalls. "My mother and I would go to the local variety store and pick out all of the projects for the summer. I always did embroidery or crochet. I had dishtowels for every day of the week. Even in Vacation Bible School, we used to do embroidery."

With a remembering smile, Paula adds,

"Growing up, we didn't have a lot of money, but the ladies liked the nice things, so they made them. Mother would go to town and look at the dresses in the windows, then go home and make them. She had no pattern. I still have some of those dresses."

Inspired by maternal patience and steady guidance, Paula became a talented seamstress herself and says that she'd like to try her hand at designing Victorian-style fashions someday. "I'd love to design children's clothes and wedding dresses." For now, Paula's fashion designing is confined to the canvas, where she paints elaborate, authentically detailed Victorian ensembles that she composes in her head as she works.

Paula still remembers when she first began falling in love with quilts and their limitless design options. "When I was a little girl, my grandmother sat me on the floor with all the quilt pieces and she said, 'You can put these colors together any way you want.' It was so much fun!"

With a warmth that draws you closer, she recounts the stories behind some of her own favorite quilts, like the Kitty Cats in a Basket quilt that her grandmother pieced for her before she got married. It was made from Paula's old skirt tails! There's also her beloved Double Wedding Ring Quilt, which she frequently incorporates into her paintings. The lovely cover-up was a gift from her in-laws. Her Rose of Sharon quilt became a heartfelt wedding gift to a dear friend — after she'd painted it, of course!

She says, "The softest quilt I ever felt is a Heart quilt that I found at a flea market quite a few years ago. I intended to keep it for my granddaughter, but I keep it in my studio and on those nights when I work late, I'll pull it up over me and sleep on the couch. I've totally worn that thing out!"

Paula has an appliquéd quilt that's covered with dogwoods. She says it shows the prettiest quilting she's ever seen. "It doesn't have any definite pattern, but the quilting on it is so gorgeous." And then, there's her Friendship quilt, which was originally presented to a Mississippi preacher by the ladies of the congregation upon his arrival at a new Baptist church. The hand-stitched cover was lovingly embellished with their decidedly Southern names.

Quilts, sewing, and embroidery are all art forms that Paula admires just as much as painting.

Her introduction to painting can be credited to her sister-in-law, who believed Paula had to be artistic, since both of her brothers were talented artists. "I had never really done any painting," Paula explains.

"She [the sister-in-law] came over one day and we struggled through a piece. She knew I was hooked after that. I still have some of those early paintings. You could finish one in an hour back then," she remembers. "You just took a pallet knife and globbed the paint on!"

Reminiscing about her early experiences, Paula recalls a favorite anecdote. "My first easel was an old wooden highchair with an enamel tray that I used for both of my children. Mother bought it in 1942, during the war. It worked out really well because I could prop my painting against the back and use the tray to hold my paints." With laughter punctuating her story, Paula continues, "I had to really get that tray clean afterward, because my boys would have eaten the paint!"

It took almost fourteen years for the self-taught artist to be "discovered" by the art community. "I never used to let anyone see my work," she says with characteristic humility. "I'd only give

> "I've always felt that quilts were the way country women expressed themselves."

my paintings to Mother and Dad. Parents will hang anything!"

Luckily, Paula's parents weren't the only ones who appreciated her talent.

Early on, when she often threw away her watercolors, one of her neighbors retrieved several paintings from the trash and took them to be framed. Paula was quite surprised when the frame shop owners called and wanted to see more of her work. Reluctantly, she agreed. "One day I decided to take about five paintings in, and they sold! I couldn't believe it," she says.

In those early years, Paula's "studio" was in her living room. "When the boys were little, they just knew to stay away from my things. It was confined to such a small area. But that may have been better, because now my studio is such a mess!"

Today, her second-floor studio sits "way up in the trees" and has lots of big windows all across the back. It's from this sunny haven that Paula re-creates images of a bygone era, when women fashioned colorful patchwork quilts and tended dooryard gardens full of flowers — quiet endeavors that many of us appreciate today.

A perfectionist when it comes to her art, Paula says, "When you live with your work every day, you can become possessed by it, and when your studio is at home, you can't leave it. If something goes wrong, you're not going to sleep at night. You're going to go up there, and if it takes all night you're going to straighten the problem out."

Paula thinks of herself as "a typical Southern woman. I'm more of a country person than a Victorian person when it comes to my personal things," she says. "I suppose you'd describe my tastes as soft country, or country Victorian."

An avid antique collector, Paula finds many of the props for her paintings in out-of-the-way shops. "Most of the time when I'm out antiquing, I'm looking for something for paintings. But I never go with anything particular in mind, since I collect a lot of things."

Indeed, she does! Paula's vast assortment of nostalgic collectibles includes quilts, china pitchers, satin-bound books, a spinning wheel, and of course, a closetful of exquisite Victorian apparel.

Another subject that has made Paula such a popular artist is her beautiful florals. With a bit of pride, she says that many of the vibrant bouquets she paints are from her flower garden. She admits, however, that her husband is the real gardener in the family. "He always brings in flowers for me. And when there are pretty roses, he'll bring me a bouquet."

Paula's painting takes up much of her time, but she still manages to find time for herself. To relax, she likes to grab a cup of coffee and sit in her porch swing. "I'm really not a hard person to please."

Paula takes her success one day at a time. "God has just blessed me so much, and once it's over, that's fine. It's just a special gift He's given me. This is something fun and great in life, and when it's over, it's over. But as long as He's with me and guides me, I feel like I'm in good shape whatever I do."

CONTENTS

INTRODUCING PAULA VAUGHAN....................3

ROMANTIC WEDDING RING..........................8
   Double Wedding Ring Quilt
   Double Wedding Ring Wall Hanging

CRAZY ABOUT BLUE 12
   Heartwarming Crazy Quilt
   Crazy Flanged Pillow
   Crazy Heart Pillow
   Tea Cozy
   Coaster

THE BEAUTY OF PINK 16
   New York Beauty Quilt

STITCHED WITH LOVE 18
   Hand's Work
   Papercut Pillow A
   Papercut Pillow B
   Heart Pillow

DARLING BASKETS....................................22
   Basket Quilt

A WORLD OF FLOWERS.............................24
Trip Around the World Quilt
Trip Around the World Lap Quilt

COUNTRY FAVORITE 28
Rose of Sharon Quilt

WILD ROSES 30
Wild Rose Bouquet Quilt
Nosegay Valance
Rosy Table Topper
Pillow Shams

DAINTY DRESDEN.............................34
Dresden Plate Quilt

GARDEN WEDDING.............................36
Garden Wedding Quilt
Wedding Day Wall Hanging

SPRINGTIME FLOWER BASKETS 40
Tulip Basket Quilt

LULLABY ROSES 42
Bed of Roses Quilt
Bed of Roses Baby Quilt

PROJECT INSTRUCTIONS.............................46

GENERAL INSTRUCTIONS 108

ROMANTIC WEDDING RING

*E*mbracing both something
old and something new,
the Double Wedding Ring quilt
was traditionally a bride's most
cherished matrimonial gift.
Paula's own beloved quilt
frequently appears in her
paintings. The classic design
is one of the most often-pieced
quilts in America, but the pretty
curves also make it one of the
most challenging to create.
We've simplified the pattern
by using time-saving rotary
cutting and strip piecing, along
with traditional templates. The
open areas are enhanced with
charming quilted flowers.

Instructions begin on page 46.

*I*n a more genteel time, the Double Wedding Ring pattern, symbolizing the devotion of marriage, would have been the showpiece of a bride's trousseau. You can re-create the romance of the traditional quilt in a fraction of the time with our sweet wall hanging! Pieced in soft pastels, it's made using four rings from the basic design and a simple quilting pattern.

CRAZY ABOUT BLUE

*P*aula's favorite things include vintage china and Victorian crazy quilts. Inspired by these collectibles, our Heartwarming Crazy Quilt is made by randomly sewing fabrics and edgings to a muslin square and rotary cutting the pieces to size. The assembled blocks are adorned with buttons, lacy appliqués, silk ribbon embroidery, and other trims. For a nostalgic touch, include materials that will bring to mind your own precious memories.

Instructions begin on page 51.

Sweeten the tradition of afternoon tea and conversation with this winsome ensemble. Our pretty tea cozy is embellished with golden charms and old-fashioned quilter's yo-yos. A lace-trimmed coaster completes the setting.

*I*t's the personal touches in unexpected places that characterize Paula's paintings. Simple gestures, like our crazy-quilt throw pillows, bestow a cordial welcome to those who would visit awhile. Heartwarming accents, the cushions are enhanced with lovely embroidery, ribbons, and lace.

THE BEAUTY OF PINK

*E*nlivening a room with a sense of springtime and romance, Paula's paintings often take their cue from Mother Nature's spectacular palette. We, too, followed her lead in choosing this antique New York Beauty quilt, a bold combination of curves and triangles. The radiant design is a masterpiece of stitching talent and creativity, and as in years past, completion of this quilt is a milestone achievement for a quilter. For a pretty finish, the cover shown here features an outer border of white triangles and pink teardrops.

STITCHED WITH LOVE

*A*mong the simpler pastimes of Paula's childhood, the long-cherished art of papercutting provided many hours of carefree entertainment. Chains of paper dolls, fanciful snowflakes, and lacy heart garlands often fell from her scissors, revealing the first glimpses of Paula's artistry. Quilters used the same time-tested technique for cutting folded paper patterns such as these on our album-block wall hanging and appliquéd pillows. The nostalgic accents make endearing wedding or friendship gifts.

Instructions begin on page 62.

Whatsoever thy hand findeth to do, Do it with thy might.

Ecclesiastes 9:10

DARLING
BASKETS

As a little girl, Paula spent almost every weekend at her grandparents' country home. She fondly recalls the important role baskets played in everyday rural life, from gathering eggs to picking flowers or storing needle and thread — sometimes even holding the wardrobe of doll clothes her mother sewed for her. Familiar images, like baskets, often inspired quilters' creations, and there was a time when no quilt collection would have been complete without at least one Basket quilt. The feminine pattern was a favorite of little girls, but it was equally loved by women of all ages. Then, as now, blue and white was a prized color combination.

22

Instructions begin on page 67.

A WORLD OF FLOWERS

aula loves to travel, but there's no place in the world she'd rather be than on her own cozy verandah surrounded by beautiful flowers. Cheery and efficient in its use of colorful scraps, our Trip Around the World quilt and lap quilt are assembled using rotary-cut, strip-pieced sets. We accented the concentric rows with simple grid quilting and blanket-stitch edging along the outer row.

Instructions begin on page 71.

COUNTRY FAVORITE

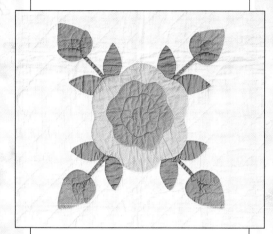

*A*s families moved about setting up new homesteads, a country woman could carry only a few personal possessions, among which you'd surely find a favorite quilt and cuttings from her prized Rose of Sharon bush. Like those resilient ladies, the plant was beautiful yet strong and hardy. Paula followed that tradition when she planted more than 30 antique roses around Giggleswick Cottage, her mountain vacation home. Profusions of their fragrant blossoms are often the subject of Paula's vibrant still lifes. The appliquéd roses on this pretty quilt also keep with tradition, presenting layered blooms with distinctive leaves, buds, and stems.

Instructions begin on page 77.

WILD ROSES

*P*aula's love for flowers has roots in her grandmother's old-fashioned country garden, where daffodils, irises, and of course, wild roses treated the senses to heady fragrances and glorious colors. The romance and unhurried charm of a beloved garden blooms to life on this fabulously feminine ensemble for the boudoir. Appliquéd quilts such as this one were considered "best quilts" in earlier days because of the time and attention to detail taken in making them. We saved time by rotary cutting the pieces for our Square-Within-A-Square variation blocks.

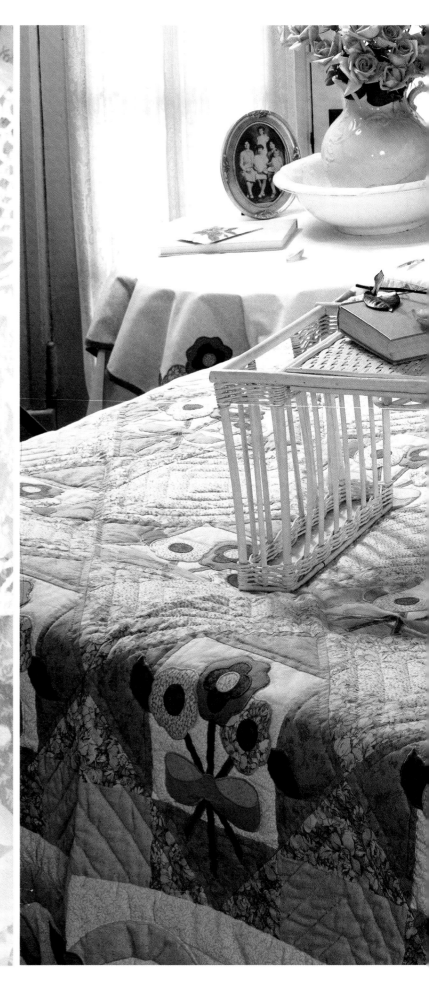

Instructions begin on page 81.

ributes to gentility, these beribboned bouquets mirror the sweet, simple image of a woman's softer nature. Fashioned using fabrics from our quilt, the matching accents are easy to embellish with fused-on appliqués and machine satin stitching. Our rose-trimmed table topper is a pretty way to invite romance to stay awhile, and the lovely valance frames the scene with plump appliquéd roses.

DAINTY DRESDEN

*E*namored by antiques,
Paula is especially fond
of old-fashioned dinnerware
that graces the table with lavish
floral prints. How appropriate
that one of her favorite quilts,
the Dresden Plate, echoes her
enchantment with china.
During the '20's, quilters were
so inspired by the dainty
scalloped edges and brilliant
hues of Germany's famous
Dresden china that they
re-created its elegance through
the Dresden Plate pattern. For
our jewel-tone version of this
classic design, we developed a
quick method to eliminate the
raw edges of the "plates."

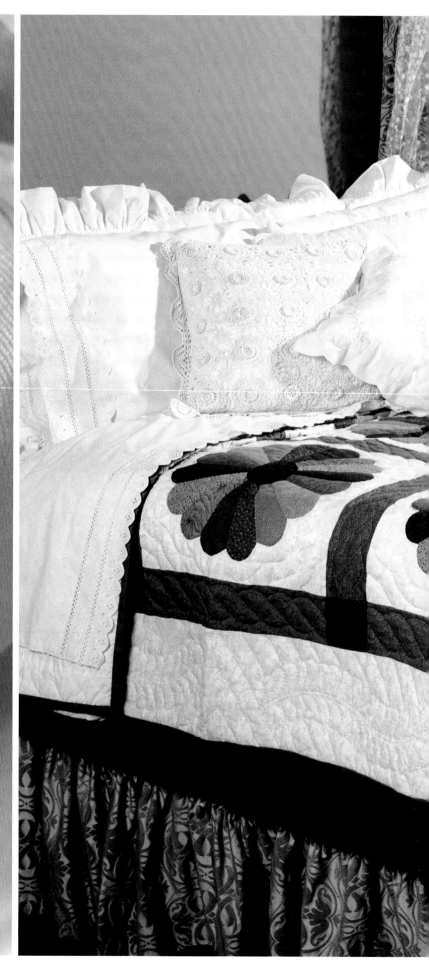

34

Instructions begin on page 88.

GARDEN WEDDING

*T*o find inspiration for her romantic paintings, Paula need look no further than her own 35-year marriage to Tommy, her high school sweetheart. He often surprises her with fresh cuttings from their flower garden, especially pretty roses, which are Paula's favorites. Stylized blossoms also unfold along the crisscrossing path of our Garden Wedding quilt. Resembling a trail of stepping stones, the elements are easy to assemble using a variety of strip-pieced units. Symbols of the love that will bloom along the couple's wedded path, the flowers are made with basic Nine-Patch blocks.

Instructions begin on page 92.

    A tribute to lasting love, this symbolic wall hanging is a heartwarming remembrance of a couple's wedding day. The center motifs are simply fused in place and appliquéd using clear nylon thread. The verse, names, and date are "stitched" on the golden rings using a permanent fabric marking pen.

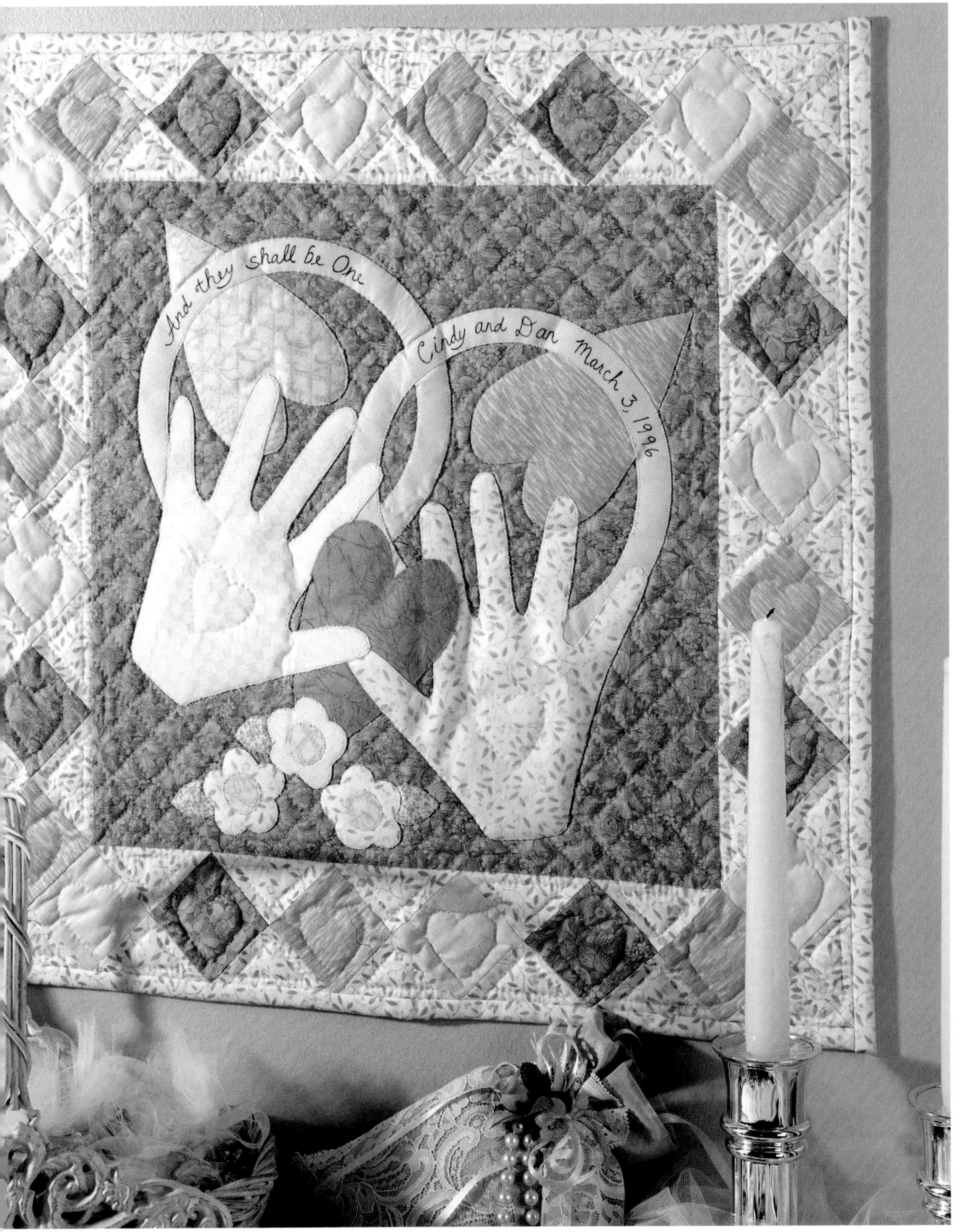
And they shall be One
Cindy and Dan March 3, 1996

SPRINGTIME FLOWER BASKETS

*A*ccomplished
needlewomen
and artists in their own right,
Paula's grandmothers certainly
would have appreciated the
uncomplicated beauty of our
Tulip Basket Quilt. The classic
appliquéd cover is reminiscent
of the 1930's kit quilts that
offered time-saving pre-matched,
and sometimes pre-cut, fabrics.
Inspired by the simple pieces
and bright pastels of our modest
tulip basket variation, you'll
have this quilt blooming
to life in no time!

Instructions begin on page 99.

LULLABY ROSES

*W*hen we first met Paula many years ago, we were fascinated by the notion of transforming her sentimental images into cross stitch designs. For her needlework fans, the charming pattern on these quilts brings to mind the squares of a cross stitch chart. Our precious *Lullaby Roses* collection includes a full-size quilt to please your budding little miss and a snuggly crib quilt to escort Baby to Dreamland on a bed of roses. Both of these sweet covers take advantage of quick rotary-cutting and strip-piecing methods.

42

Instructions begin on page 103.

44

ROMANTIC WEDDING RING

DOUBLE WEDDING RING QUILT

RING SIZE: 18" diameter
QUILT SIZE: 96" x 109"

YARDAGE REQUIREMENTS
Yardage is based on 45"w fabric.

- 8½ yards **total** of assorted pastel prints
- 6½ yards of white solid
- ⅝ yard of peach solid
- ⅝ yard of green solid
  8¾ yards for backing
  1¼ yards for binding
  120" x 120" batting

ROTARY CUTTING
All measurements include a ¼" seam allowance. Follow Rotary Cutting, page 110, to cut fabric.

1. From pastel prints:
   - Cut a total of 26 selvage-to-selvage **narrow strips** 2½"w.
   - Cut a total of 52 selvage-to-selvage **wide strips** 4¼"w.
2. From peach solid:
   - Cut 8 selvage-to-selvage strips 2½"w. From these strips, cut 127 squares 2½" x 2½".
3. From green solid:
   - Cut 8 selvage-to-selvage strips 2½"w. From these strips, cut 127 squares 2½" x 2½".

ASSEMBLING THE STRIP SETS
Follow Piecing and Pressing, page 112, to make strip sets.

1. Beginning and ending with **narrow strips**, assemble 2 **narrow** and 4 **wide strips** in random color order to make Strip Set. Make 13 **Strip Sets**.

Strip Set (make 13)

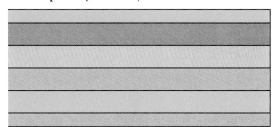

TEMPLATE CUTTING
Use patterns AA, AB, C, and D, page 50, and follow Template Cutting, page 112, to cut fabric.

1. From 4 **Strip Sets**, use **Template AA** to cut out 254 **AA Units**, placing center line of template on seams as shown in **Fig. 1**.

Fig. 1

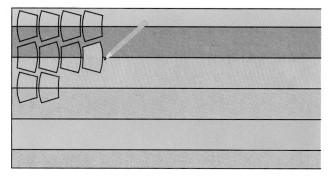

2. From remaining 9 **Strip Sets**, use **Template AB** to cut out 254 **AB Units** and 254 **Reversed AB Units**, placing center line of template on seams.
3. From white solid, cut 127 **C's** using **Template C** and 56 **D's** using **Template D**.

ASSEMBLING THE QUILT TOP
Follow Piecing and Pressing, page 112, to make quilt top.

1. Assemble 1 **Reversed AB Unit**, 1 **AA Unit**, and 1 **AB Unit** to make Unit 1. Make 254 **Unit 1's**.

Unit 1 (make 254)

2. Assemble 2 **squares** and 1 **Unit 1** to make Unit 2. Make 127 **Unit 2's**.

Unit 2 (make 127)

3. (*Note:* For curved seams in Steps 3 - 8, match centers and pin at center and at dots, then match and pin between these points. Sew seam with convex edge on bottom next to feed dogs.) Assemble 1 **C** and 1 **Unit 1** to make Unit 3. Make 127 **Unit 3's**.

Unit 3 (make 127)

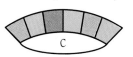

4. Assemble 1 **Unit 2** and 1 **Unit 3** to make Unit 4. Make 127 **Unit 4's**.

Unit 4 (make 127)

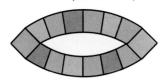

5. Assemble 4 Unit 4's and 1 D to make Unit 5. Make 28 Unit 5's.

Unit 5 (make 28)

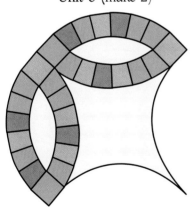

D

6. Assemble 2 Unit 4's and 1 D to make Unit 6. Make 2 Unit 6's.

Unit 6 (make 2)

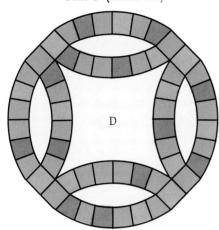

7. Assemble 1 Unit 4 and 1 D to make Unit 7. Make 11 Unit 7's.

Unit 7 (make 11)

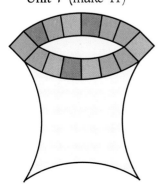

8. Follow Assembly Diagram to assemble Unit 5's, Unit 6's, Unit 7's, and remaining D's into horizontal Rows. Assemble Rows to complete Quilt Top.

COMPLETING THE QUILT

1. Follow Quilting, page 117, to mark, layer, and quilt, using Quilting Diagram as a suggestion. Our quilt is hand quilted.
2. Cut a 42" square of binding fabric. Follow Making Continuous Bias Strip Binding, page 121, to make approximately 14 yds of 2½"w bias binding.
3. Follow Steps 1 and 2 of Attaching Binding with Mitered Corners, page 122, to pin binding to front of quilt. Sew binding to quilt, easing curves and leaving a 2" overlap. Trim off excess binding and stitch overlap in place. Fold binding over to quilt backing and pin in place, covering stitching line. Blindstitch binding to backing.

Quilt Top Diagram

Quilting Diagram

47

DOUBLE WEDDING RING WALL HANGING

RING SIZE: 18" diameter
WALL HANGING SIZE: 31" x 31"

YARDAGE REQUIREMENTS
Yardage is based on 45"w fabric.

■ 1¾ yards **total** of assorted pastel prints
□ 1 yard of white solid
▨ ⅛ yard of peach print
▨ ⅛ yard of blue print
1¼ yards for backing and hanging sleeve
¾ yard for binding
35" x 35" batting

ROTARY CUTTING
All measurements include a ¼" seam allowance. Follow Rotary Cutting, page 110, to cut fabric.

1. From pastel prints: ◩
   - Cut a total of 2 selvage-to-selvage strips 2½"w.
   - Cut a total of 5 selvage-to-selvage strips 4¼"w.

2. From peach print: ▨
   - Cut 1 selvage-to-selvage strip 2½"w. From this strip, cut 12 squares 2½" x 2½".

3. From blue print: ▨
   - Cut 1 selvage-to-selvage strip 2½"w. From this strip, cut 12 squares 2½" x 2½".

ASSEMBLING THE WALL HANGING TOP
Follow Piecing and Pressing, page 112, to make wall hanging top.

1. Beginning and ending with narrow strips, assemble strips in random color order to make 1 **Strip Set**.

Strip Set (make 1)

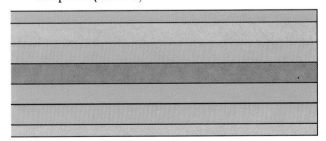

2. Referring to Steps 1 and 2 of **Template Cutting** for Double Wedding Ring Quilt, page 46, cut 24 **AA Units**, 24 **AB Units**, and 24 **Reversed AB Units** from **Strip Set**. From white solid, cut 12 **C's** using **Template C** and 4 **D's** using **Template D**.

3. Follow Steps 1 - 4 of **Assembling the Quilt Top** for Double Wedding Ring Quilt, page 46, to make 12 **Unit 4's**.

4. Follow Steps 5 and 6 of **Assembling the Quilt Top** for Double Wedding Ring Quilt, page 47, to make 2 **Unit 5's** and 2 **Unit 6's**.

5. Assemble **Unit 5's** and **Unit 6's** to complete **Wall Hanging Top**.

COMPLETING THE WALL HANGING

1. Follow **Quilting**, page 117, to mark, layer, and quilt, using **Quilting Diagram** as a suggestion. Our wall hanging is hand quilted.

2. Cut a 22" square of binding fabric. Follow **Making Continuous Bias Strip Binding**, page 121, to make approximately 5 yds of 2½"w bias binding.

3. Follow Step 3 of **Completing the Quilt** for Double Wedding Ring Quilt, page 47, to attach binding to wall hanging.

Wall Hanging Top Diagram

Quilting Diagram

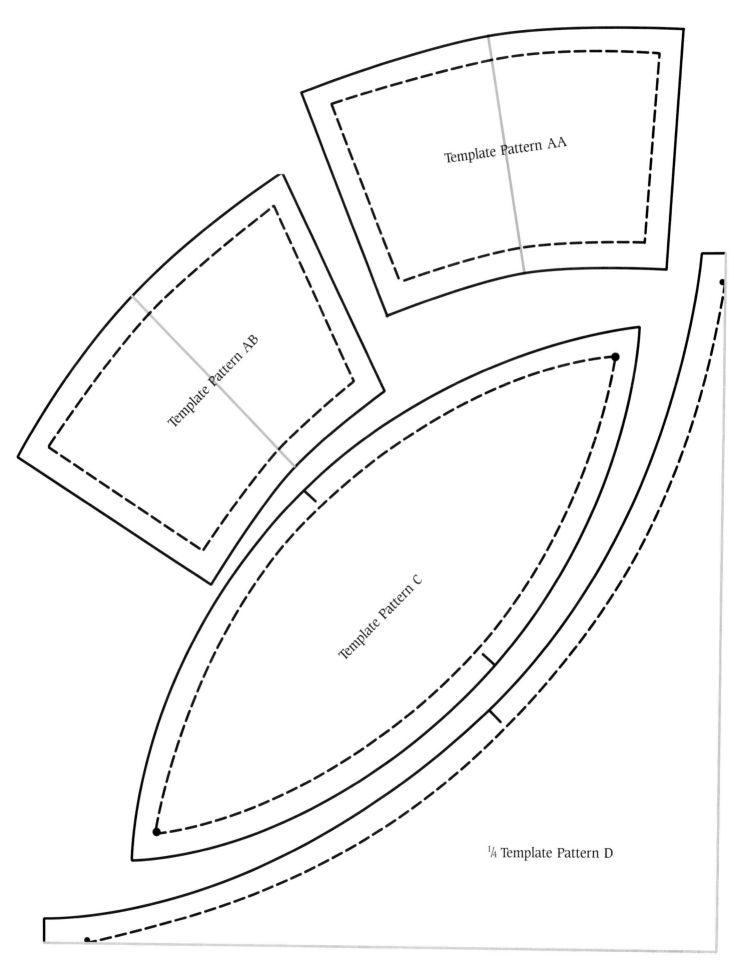

Template Pattern AA

Template Pattern AB

Template Pattern C

¹/₄ Template Pattern D

50

CRAZY ABOUT BLUE

HEARTWARMING CRAZY QUILT

BLOCK SIZE: 9" x 9"
WALL HANGING SIZE: 33" x 33"

YARDAGE REQUIREMENTS
Yardage is based on 45"w fabric.

- 2 yards of blue print for border, backing, and hanging sleeve
- 2 yards **total** of assorted blue and white print scraps
- 1 yard of muslin for foundations
- 1 square 9" x 9" of white solid
- 4⅛ yards of 1"w embroidered lace for border
- 35" x 35" batting

You will also need:

items and trims for embellishment (we used embroidery floss, silk ribbon, pieces of lace and ribbon, beads, buttons, charms, fabric yo-yos, and doilies)

CUTTING OUT THE PIECES
All measurements include a ¼" seam allowance. Follow Rotary Cutting, page 110, to cut fabric.

1. From blue print:
   - Cut 4 borders 3¾" x 37".
   - Cut 1 backing 35" x 35".
   - Cut 1 hanging sleeve 7" x 33".

2. From muslin:
   - Cut 3 strips 9"w. From these strips, cut 9 foundation squares 9" x 9".

PIECING THE BLOCKS
1. From 1 of the fabric scraps, cut a five-sided piece. Place this piece, right side up, on 1 foundation square (Fig. 1).

Fig. 1

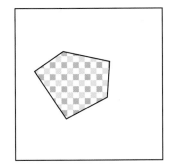

2. Referring to **Figs.** 2 and 3, place a second piece on the first, matching right sides and one straight raw edge. Stitch ¼" from matched raw edges, stitching through all layers. Flip second piece to right side and press.

Fig. 2

Fig. 3

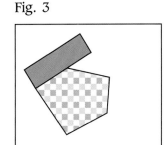

3. Referring to **Figs.** 4 - 12, continue to add pieces, stitch, flip, and press until pieces extend at least ¼" past all edges of **foundation square**.

Fig. 4

Fig. 5

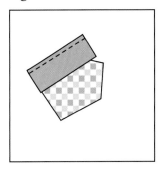

Fig. 6

Fig. 7

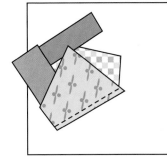
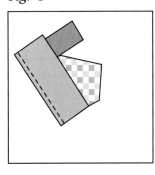
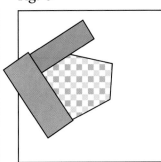
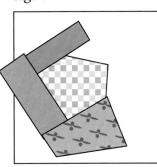

Fig. 8

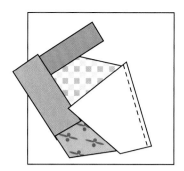

Fig. 9

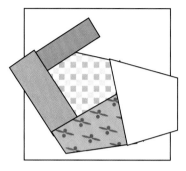

Fig. 10

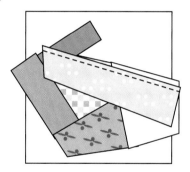

Fig. 11

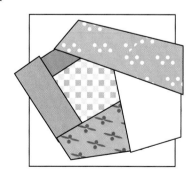

Fig. 12

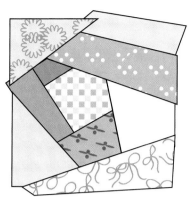

4. Place pieced square, right side down, on cutting mat. Use rotary cutter and ruler to trim off crazy piecing ¼" outside **foundation square** (**Fig. 13**) to complete **Block**.

Fig. 13

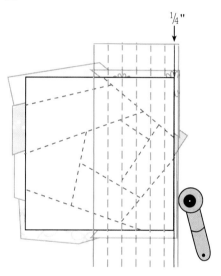

5. Repeat Steps 1 - 4 to make a total of 9 **Blocks**.

Block (make 9)

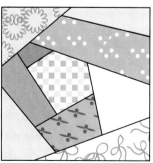

EMBELLISHING THE BLOCKS

Refer to photo and use the following suggestions to embellish the pieced blocks.

- Using pattern, page 56, trace **Small Heart** outline on white solid square. Using **Embroidery Diagram**, page 56, as a suggestion, follow **Embroidery Stitches**, page 124, to embroider heart. Cut out heart ¼" outside drawn line. Press ¼" seam allowance to wrong side. Use blindstitch to appliqué heart to center of one pieced block. Hand or machine stitch narrow lace around edge of heart.
- Use embroidery floss and/or silk ribbon and follow **Embroidery Stitches**, page 124, to add embroidery to seamlines or individual patches.
- Machine or hand stitch lace, ribbon, or other trim along seamlines. Use seam ripper to remove a few stitches at end of adjoining seamline; insert raw end of trim into opening. Blindstitch opening closed.
- Sew on buttons, charms, and beads.
- Use small pieces of crochet or tatting (doilies or sections salvaged from worn pieces), enclosing any cut edges in a seamline to prevent raveling.
- To make each fabric yo-yo, cut a 3½" dia. circle from desired fabric. Turn raw edge of circle ¼" to wrong side. Using a double strand of quilting thread, work a **Running Stitch**, page 125, along turned edge. Pull ends of thread to tightly gather circle; knot thread securely and trim ends. Flatten circle. Sew on yo-yos, either by stitching through a button in the center of yo-yo or by blindstitching edges to block.

ASSEMBLING THE WALL HANGING TOP

Follow **Piecing and Pressing**, *page 112, to make wall hanging top.*

1. Sew 3 **Blocks** together to make row. Make 3 rows. Sew rows together to complete center section of wall hanging.
2. Cut lace for border into 4 equal pieces. Matching long raw edge of lace to one long raw edge of **border**, baste 1 piece of lace, right side up, to right side of 1 **border**. Repeat with remaining lace pieces and **borders**.
3. Follow **Adding Mitered Borders**, page 117, to sew borders to center section to complete **Wall Hanging Top**.

COMPLETING THE WALL HANGING

1. Center backing fabric, right side up, on batting. With right sides together, center wall hanging top on backing. Working from center outward, smooth out any wrinkles and use safety pins to pin layers together approximately every 6". Use straight pins to pin edges of layers together. Trim batting and backing to same size as wall hanging top.

2. Using a ½" seam allowance and leaving a 12" opening for turning, sew layers together. Trim corners, remove all pins, and turn wall hanging right side out. Sew final closure by hand.
3. To quilt wall hanging, refer to **Quilting**, page 117, to hand or machine quilt in the ditch between blocks and around inside edge of border.
4. Add additional embellishment to seamlines between blocks, if desired.
5. Press short edges of **hanging sleeve** ¼" to wrong side. Press ¼" to wrong side again and stitch along first fold. Matching right sides and raw edges, stitch ¼" from raw edges to form a tube. Turn right side out and press.
6. Center sleeve 1" below top edge of wall hanging back. Hand stitch both long edges to wall hanging backing, taking care not to stitch through to front of wall hanging.

Wall Hanging Top Diagram

CRAZY HEART PILLOW

PILLOW SIZE: 11" x 13" (including ruffle)

SUPPLIES

9" x 9" piece of muslin for foundation square
scraps of blue and white print fabrics
9" x 9" square for pillow back
4½" x 66" fabric strip (pieced as necessary) for ruffle
items and trims for embellishment (we used embroidery floss, silk ribbon, pieces of lace and ribbon, beads, buttons, charms, and doilies)
polyester fiberfill
tracing paper

MAKING THE PILLOW

1. Using foundation square and fabric scraps, follow **Piecing the Blocks**, page 51, to make 1 **Block**.
2. To make pattern for **Pillow Top**, fold tracing paper in half. Place fold on grey line of **Large Heart** pattern, page 55; trace. Cut out pattern; unfold. Position pattern on **Block**; draw around pattern. Do not cut out.
3. Refer to **Embellishing the Blocks**, page 53, to embellish **Block** within the drawn heart shape as desired.
4. Cut out **Pillow Top** ½" outside drawn heart shape.
5. Follow **Pillow Finishing**, page 123, to finish pillow with ruffle.

CRAZY FLANGED PILLOW

PILLOW SIZE: 13" x 13" (including flange)

SUPPLIES

9" x 9" piece of muslin for **foundation square**
scraps of blue and white print fabrics
9" x 9" square of white fabric for heart appliqué
1 yard of narrow lace
4 strips 2" x 16" of blue print for pillow top **borders**
1⅛ yards of 1"w embroidered lace
13½" x 13½" square of fabric for **pillow back**
items and trims for embellishment (we used embroidery floss, silk ribbon, pieces of lace and ribbon, beads, buttons, charms, and doilies)
polyester fiberfill

MAKING THE PILLOW

1. Using **foundation square** and fabric scraps, follow **Piecing the Blocks**, page 51, to make 1 **Block**.
2. Refer to **Embellishing the Blocks**, page 53, to add heart appliqué and other embellishments to **Block** as desired.
3. Follow Steps 2 and 3 of **Assembling the Wall Hanging Top**, page 53, to add **borders** to **Block** to complete **Pillow Top**.
4. Place **Pillow Top** and **pillow back** right sides together. Leaving an opening for turning, stitch ¼" from raw edge. Clip corners; turn right side out.
5. Leaving a 2"w opening on same side as opening for turning, stitch in the ditch between **Block** and border (**Fig. 1**). Stuff pillow with fiberfill. Sew both openings closed.

Fig. 1

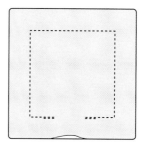

TEA COZY AND COASTER

SUPPLIES

2 rectangles 15" x 20" of blue print fabric
2 rectangles 15" x 20" of lining fabric
2 rectangles 15" x 20" of batting
2 squares 4½" x 4½" of blue print fabric
1 square 4½" x 4½" of batting
1 yard of 2½"w bias fabric strip for binding
items and trims for embellishment (we used embroidery floss, silk ribbon, pieces of lace and ribbon, beads, buttons, charms, and doilies)
tracing paper

MAKING THE TEA COZY AND COASTER

1. To make pattern for tea cozy, fold tracing paper in half. Place fold on grey line of pattern, page 55; trace. Cut out pattern; unfold.
2. Use pattern to cut two pieces each from blue print fabric, lining fabric, and batting.
3. To make cozy front, place 1 blue print piece right side up on 1 batting piece; baste close to edges. Refer to photo and **Embellishing the Blocks**, page 53, to embellish cozy front as desired.
4. To assemble cozy front and lining, match edges and place 1 lining piece and cozy front right sides together. Using a ½" seam allowance, stitch through all layers along bottom edges only. Turn right side out and press. Using remaining fabric and batting pieces, repeat to make cozy back.
5. With lining sides facing, place cozy front and back together; baste all layers together along raw edges.
6. Use bias fabric strip and follow Steps 4 and 5 of **Attaching Binding with Overlapped Corners**, page 122, to bind raw edges of tea cozy.
7. To make coaster, place 1 fabric square on batting square to make coaster top. Referring to **Embellishing the Blocks**, page 53, embellish coaster top as desired.
8. Place coaster top and remaining fabric square wrong sides together; baste along raw edges.
9. Use bias fabric strip and follow **Attaching Binding with Mitered Corners**, page 122, to bind coaster.

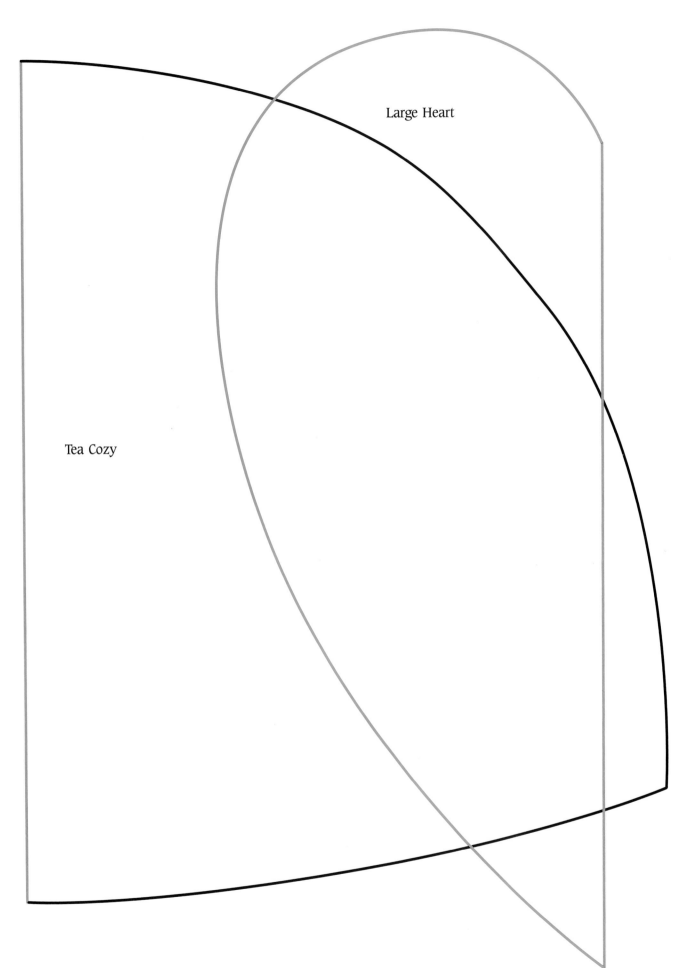

Large Heart

Tea Cozy

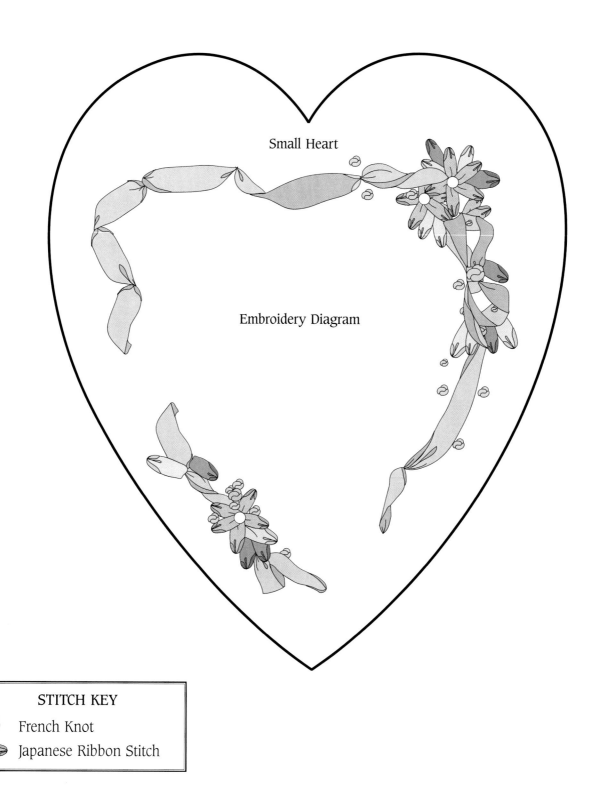

Small Heart

Embroidery Diagram

STITCH KEY

French Knot

Japanese Ribbon Stitch

THE BEAUTY OF PINK

NEW YORK BEAUTY QUILT

BLOCK SIZE: 15¾" x 15¾"
QUILT SIZE: 93" x 93"

YARDAGE REQUIREMENTS
Yardage is based on 45"w fabric.

☐ 7½ yards of ecru solid

☐ 6 yards of pink solid

☐ 2¾ yards of green solid
8⅝ yards for backing
1 yard for binding
120" x 120" batting

CUTTING OUT THE PIECES
All measurements include a ¼" seam allowance. Use patterns, pages 60-61, and follow Template Cutting, page 112, to cut fabric.

1. From pink solid: ☐
   - Cut 576 A's.
   - Cut 64 D's.
   - Cut 1004 F's.
   - Cut 9 G's.
   - Cut 144 L's.

2. From ecru solid: ☐
   - Cut 512 B's.
   - Cut 16 E's.
   - Cut 952 F's.
   - Cut 36 H's.
   - Cut 4 J's.
   - Cut 136 K's.

3. From green solid: ☐
   - Cut 64 C's.
   - Cut 36 I's.
   - Cut 24 sashing strips 2½" x 16¼".
   - Cut 2 side borders 2½" x 81½".
   - Cut 2 top/bottom borders 2½" x 85½".

ASSEMBLING THE QUILT TOP
Follow Piecing and Pressing, page 112, to make quilt top.

1. Sew 8 B's and 9 A's together to make Unit 1. Make 64 Unit 1's.

Unit 1 (make 64)

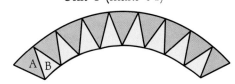

2. (*Note:* For the curved seams in Steps 1-4, match centers and pin at center and at dots, then match and pin between these points. Sew seam with convex edge on bottom next to feed dogs. When joining Units, do not sew into seam allowances; begin and end stitching ¼" from raw edges.) Sew 1 Unit 1 to 1 C to make Unit 2. Make 64 Unit 2's.

Unit 2 (make 64)

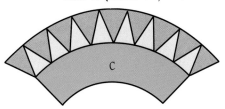

3. Sew 1 Unit 2 and 1 D together to make Unit 3. Make 64 Unit 3's. Trim outer straight edge of triangles on Unit 3's even with edges of C and D.

Unit 3 (make 64)

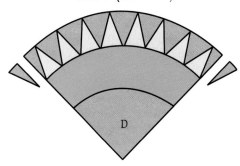

4. Sew 4 Unit 3's and 1 E together to complete Block. Make 16 Blocks.

Block (make 16)

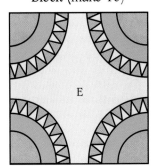

5. For sashing, sew 14 ecru F's and 15 pink F's together to make **Unit 4**. Make 48 **Unit 4's**.

Unit 4 (make 48)

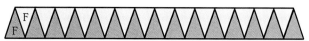

6. Sew 1 **sashing strip** and 2 **Unit 4's** together to make **Unit 5**. Repeat to make a total of 24 **Unit 5's**. Trim triangles on **Unit 5's** even with edges of **strip**.

Unit 5 (make 24)

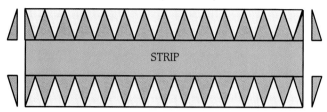

7. Sew 1 **H** and 2 **I's** together to make **Unit 6**. Make 18 **Unit 6's**. Sew 1 **G** and 2 **H's** together to make **Unit 7**. Make 9 **Unit 7's**. Sew 1 **Unit 7** and 2 **Unit 6's** together to make **Unit 8**. Make 9 **Unit 8's**.

Unit 6 (make 18)   Unit 7 (make 9)   Unit 8 (make 9)

 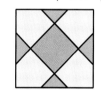

8. Sew 3 **Unit 5's** and 4 **Blocks** together to make a **Row**. Make 4 **Rows**.

Row (make 4)

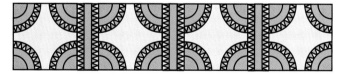

9. Sew 3 **Unit 8's** and 4 **Unit 5's** together to make **Unit 9**. Make 3 **Unit 9's**.

Unit 9 (make 3)

10. Sew **Unit 9's** and **Rows** together to make center section of quilt.

Center Section

11. Beginning and ending with a pink F, sew 70 ecru F's and 71 pink F's together to make **inner pieced border**. Make 4 **inner pieced borders**. Trim each end by cutting off ½ of the first and last pink F's (**Fig. 1**).

Fig. 1

12. Matching ecru triangles to center section, sew 1 **inner pieced border** each to top and bottom edges of center section.
13. Sew 1 **J** to each end of each remaining **inner pieced border**; sew borders to sides of center section.
14. Sew **side**, then **top** and **bottom borders** to center section.
15. Beginning and ending with an L, sew 34 K's and 35 L's together to make **Unit 10**. Make 4 **Unit 10's** to make **outer pieced borders**.

Unit 10 (make 4)

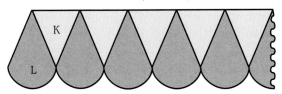

16. Sew 1 **outer pieced border** each to top, bottom, and side edges of center section. Refer to Steps 2-4 of **Working with Diamonds and Set-In Seams**, page 114, to sew one L into each corner of **outer pieced border** (Fig. 2) to complete **Quilt Top**.

Fig. 2

COMPLETING THE QUILT
1. Follow **Quilting**, page 117, to mark, layer, and quilt, using **Quilting Diagram** as a suggestion. Our quilt is hand quilted.
2. Cut a 36" square of binding fabric. Follow **Binding**, page 121, to bind quilt using 1¼"w bias binding.
3. Follow Steps 1 and 2 of **Attaching Binding with Mitered Corners**, page 122, to pin binding to front of quilt. Using a ¼" seam allowance, sew binding to quilt, easing curves and leaving a 2" overlap. Trim excess binding and stitch overlap in place. Fold binding over to quilt backing and pin in place, covering stitching line. Blindstitch binding to backing.

Quilt Top Diagram

Quilting Diagram

59

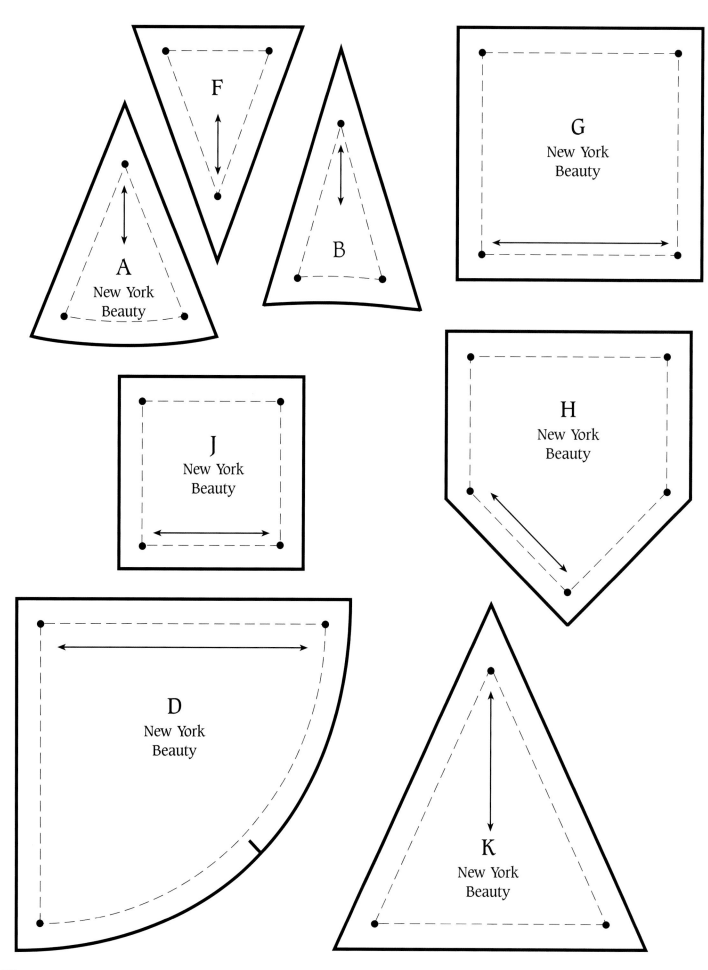

F

A
New York
Beauty

B

G
New York
Beauty

J
New York
Beauty

H
New York
Beauty

D
New York
Beauty

K
New York
Beauty

60

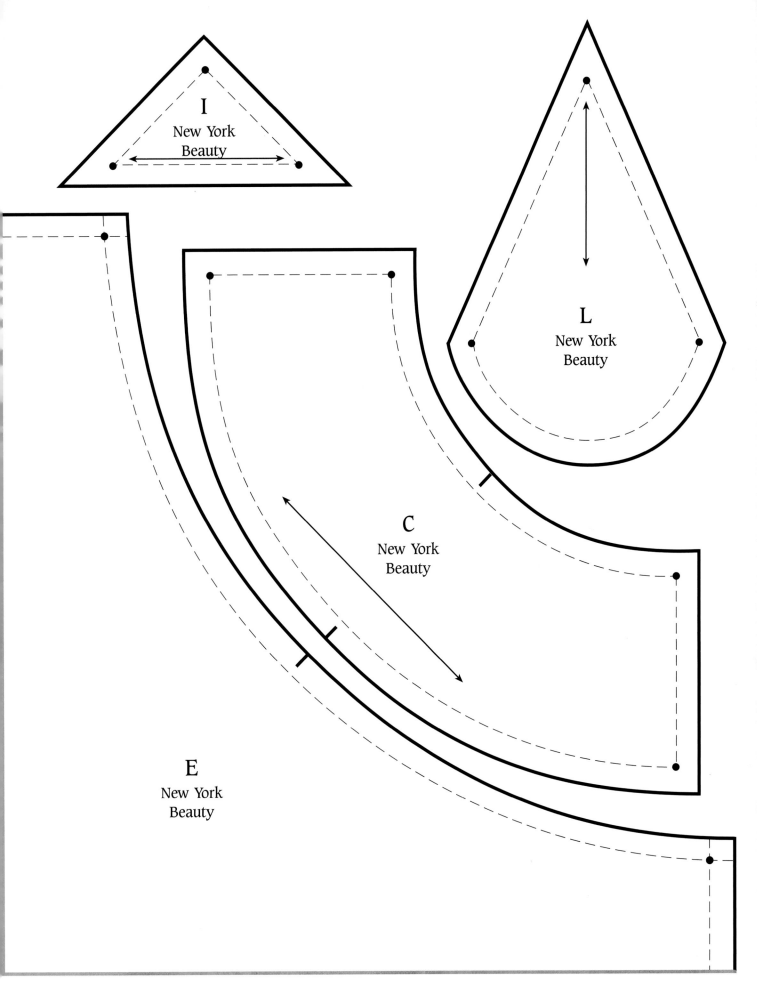

I
New York
Beauty

L
New York
Beauty

C
New York
Beauty

E
New York
Beauty

STITCHED WITH LOVE

HAND'S WORK

BLOCK SIZE: 10½" x 10½"
WALL HANGING SIZE: 30" x 30"

YARDAGE REQUIREMENTS
Yardage is based on 45"w fabric.

- ⅞ yard of light pink print
- ⅞ yard of floral print
- ⅜ yard of brown print
- ⅜ yard of dark pink print
- ⅛ yard of medium pink print
  1⅛ yards for backing and hanging sleeve
  ⅝ yard for binding
  33" x 33" batting

You will also need:
  5" x 5" square of freezer paper
  10" x 10" square of paper-backed fusible web
  transparent monofilament thread for appliqué
  permanent fabric pen

CUTTING OUT THE PIECES
All measurements include a ¼" seam allowance. Follow Rotary Cutting, page 110, to cut fabric.

1. From light pink print:
   - Cut 1 selvage-to-selvage strip 5½"w. From this strip, cut 4 **squares** 5½" x 5½".
   - Cut 2 selvage-to-selvage strips 2¼"w. From these strips, cut 32 **small squares** 2¼" x 2¼".
   - Cut 1 rectangle 12" x 18" for **triangle-squares**.

2. From floral print:
   - Cut 1 selvage-to-selvage strip 4½"w. From this strip, cut 8 squares 4½" x 4½". Cut squares once diagonally to make 16 **triangles**.
   - Cut 2 selvage-to-selvage strips 2¼"w. From these strips, cut 16 **small rectangles** 2¼" x 4".
   - Cut 1 rectangle 12" x 18" for **triangle-squares**.

3. From brown print:
   - Cut 4 selvage-to-selvage strips 3"w. From these strips, cut 12 **sashing strips** 3" x 11".

4. From dark pink print:
   - Cut 1 **large square** 10" x 10".

5. From medium pink print:
   - Cut 1 selvage-to-selvage strip 3"w. From this strip, cut 9 **sashing squares** 3" x 3".

ASSEMBLING THE WALL HANGING TOP
Follow Piecing and Pressing, page 112, to make wall hanging top.

1. To make triangle-squares, place light pink and floral **rectangles** right sides together. Referring to **Fig. 1**, follow **Making Triangle-Squares**, page 113, to make 48 **triangle-squares**.

Fig. 1

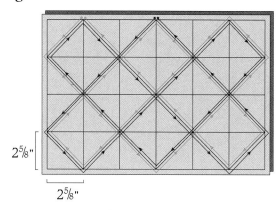

triangle-square (make 48)

2. Place 1 **small square** on 1 **small rectangle** with right sides together and stitch diagonally as shown in **Fig. 2**. Trim ¼" from stitching line as shown in **Fig. 3**. Press open, pressing seam allowance toward darker fabric.

Fig. 2   Fig. 3

 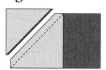

3. Place 1 **small square** on opposite end of **small rectangle**. Stitch diagonally as shown in **Fig. 4**. Trim and press open as in Step 2 to complete **Unit 1**. Make 16 **Unit 1's**.

Fig. 4   Unit 1 (make 16)

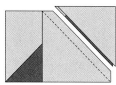 

4. Sew 2 **triangle-squares** and 1 **Unit 1** together to make **Unit 2**. Make 16 **Unit 2's**.

Unit 2 (make 16)

5. Sew 2 **triangle-squares** and 1 **Unit 2** together to make **Unit 3**. Make 8 **Unit 3**'s.

Unit 3 (make 8)

6. Sew 4 **triangles** and 1 **square** together to make **Unit 4**. Make 4 **Unit 4**'s.

Unit 4 (make 4)

7. Sew 2 **Unit 2**'s and 1 **Unit 4** together to make **Unit 5**. Make 4 **Unit 5**'s.

Unit 5 (make 4)

8. Sew 2 **Unit 3**'s and 1 **Unit 5** together to make **Block**. Make 4 **Blocks**.

Block (make 4)

9. Follow manufacturer's instructions to fuse web to wrong side of **large square**. Cut **large square** into 4 squares 5" x 5". Do not remove paper backing.

10. To make pattern for appliqué, carefully fold and crease freezer paper, shiny side in, into eighths as shown in **Figs. 2a - 2c** (dots indicate center of paper). Unfold paper and use **Papercut Pattern A**, page 65, to trace pattern onto section shaded in **Fig. 2d**.

Fig. 2a   Fig. 2b

Fig. 2c   Fig. 2d

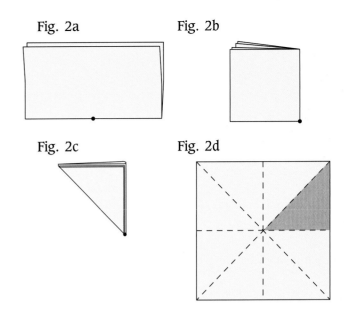

11. Refold paper and use small, sharp scissors to cut out appliqué shape, cutting away shaded sections of pattern. Unfold freezer paper pattern.

12. Center pattern, shiny side down, on wrong side of 1 fused fabric square; use a dry iron to iron pattern in place.

13. Use a sharp pencil to draw around freezer paper pattern; remove pattern. Use small, sharp scissors to carefully cut out **appliqué**. Remove paper backing.

14. Reusing freezer paper pattern each time, repeat Steps 12 and 13 to make 4 **appliqués**.

15. Follow **Invisible Appliqué**, page 115, to fuse and stitch 1 appliqué to each **Block**. Use permanent pen to write name on each block in center of **appliqué**.

16. Sew 3 **sashing squares** and 2 **sashing strips** together to make **Row A**. Make 3 **Row A**'s.

Row A (make 3)

17. Sew 3 **sashing strips** and 2 **Blocks** together to make **Row B**. Make 2 **Row B**'s.

Row B (make 2)

18. Referring to **Wall Hanging Top Diagram**, sew **Rows** together to complete **Wall Hanging Top**.

COMPLETING THE WALL HANGING

1. Follow **Quilting**, page 117, to mark, layer, and quilt, using **Quilting Diagram** as a suggestion. Our wall hanging is hand quilted.
2. Follow **Making a Hanging Sleeve**, page 123, to attach hanging sleeve to wall hanging.
3. Cut a 20" square of binding fabric. Follow **Binding**, page 121, to bind quilt using 2½"w bias binding with mitered corners.

Wall Hanging Top Diagram

Wall Hanging Quilting Diagram

PAPERCUT PILLOW A

PILLOW SIZE: 17" x 17"

SUPPLIES

10" x 10" **large square** of pink print fabric
10" x 10" square of paper-backed fusible web
5" x 5" square of freezer paper
11½" x 11½" **background square** of light pink print fabric
4 **inner borders** 1¼" x 14" of brown print fabric
4 **outer borders** 2¼" x 18" of floral print fabric
19" x 19" square of fabric for pillow top backing
19" x 19" batting
16½" x 16½" square of fabric for pillow back
2½" x 76" bias fabric strip for binding
polyester fiberfill

MAKING THE PILLOW

Follow Piecing and Pressing, page 112, to make pillow.

1. Follow Steps 10 - 14 of **Assembling the Wall Hanging Top**, page 62, to make 4 **appliqués** using **Papercut Pattern A**.
2. Arrange appliqués on **background square** and follow manufacturer's instructions to fuse in place.
3. Sew **inner borders** to top, bottom, then side edges of **background square**, trimming off remainder of each **border** after stitching. Repeat to add **outer borders** to make pillow top.
4. Follow **Quilting**, page 117, to layer and quilt pillow top. The center of our pillow top is machine quilted in a stipple pattern (see **Machine Stipple Quilting**, page 120) with in-the-ditch quilting between the borders.
5. Trim batting and backing even with pillow top. Place pillow top and pillow back wrong sides together; sew pieces together using a ¼" seam allowance and leaving an opening for stuffing. Stuff pillow with fiberfill and sew opening closed.
6. Fold bias fabric strip in half lengthwise, matching wrong sides and raw edges, and follow **Attaching Binding with Mitered Corners**, page 122, to bind pillow edges.

PAPERCUT PILLOW B

PILLOW SIZE: 16½" x 16½"

SUPPLIES
8½" x 8½" square of light pink fabric
8½" x 8½" square of paper-backed fusible web
8½" x 8½" square of freezer paper
11" x 11" **background square** of pink print fabric
4 **inner borders** 1¼" x 14" of brown print fabric
4 **outer borders** 2¼" x 18" of floral print fabric
18" x 18" square of fabric for pillow top backing
18" x 18" batting
16" x 16" square of fabric for pillow back
2½" x 72" bias fabric strip for binding
polyester fiberfill

MAKING THE PILLOW
Follow Piecing and Pressing, page 112, to make pillow.

1. Follow manufacturer's instructions to fuse web to wrong side of light pink fabric. Do not remove paper backing.
2. Use **Papercut Pattern B** and refer to Steps 10 - 13 of **Assembling the Wall Hanging Top**, page 62, to make 1 appliqué.
3. Center appliqué on **background square** and follow manufacturer's instructions to fuse in place.
4. Follow Steps 3 - 6 of **Making the Pillow**, page 124, to complete pillow.

HEART PILLOW

PILLOW SIZE: 15½" x 15½" (including ruffle)

SUPPLIES
12" x 12" square of pink print fabric
12" x 12" square of cream print fabric
12" x 12" square of paper-backed fusible web
12" x 12" square of freezer paper
1 yard of ¾"w flat lace
5½" x 80" strip of floral print fabric (pieced as necessary) for ruffle
80" of 2"w flat lace
½"w purchased pink ribbon rose
¼ yard of ⅛"w light pink satin ribbon
¼ yard of ¼"w pink satin ribbon
permanent fabric marking pen
polyester fiberfill

MAKING THE PILLOW
1. Place freezer paper, shiny side down, over **Lacy Heart Pattern**, page 66, and trace.
2. Use a dry iron to iron freezer paper, shiny side down, to wrong side of cream print square. Use fabric marking pen to trace design onto right side of cream print square. Remove freezer paper.
3. Center web square, web side down, over **Lacy Heart Pattern** and trace outer solid outline of heart only. Follow manufacturer's instructions to fuse web to wrong side of pink print square. Carefully cut out heart shape, leaving outer portion of square intact. Remove paper backing.
4. Layer cream print square and pink print square, right sides up, centering heart cutout over heart design. Follow manufacturer's instructions to fuse layers together.
5. Position ¾"w lace around heart, aligning edge of lace with raw edge of heart cutout. Use a narrow zigzag stitch to stitch around heart to secure edges of lace and heart cutout.
6. Trim square to measure 11" x 11" to make **Pillow Top.**
7. Use 5½" x 80" fabric strip and follow Step 2 of **Adding Ruffle to Pillow Top**, page 124, to prepare fabric strip. Repeat using 2"w lace.
8. Aligning raw edges of fabric strip with one edge of 2"w lace, follow Steps 3 and 4 of **Adding Ruffle to Pillow Top** to make ruffle and baste to pillow top.
9. Follow **Pillow Finishing**, page 123, to make pillow.
10. Tie ribbons into a small bow. Tack bow to pillow; tack ribbon rose over bow know to complete pillow.

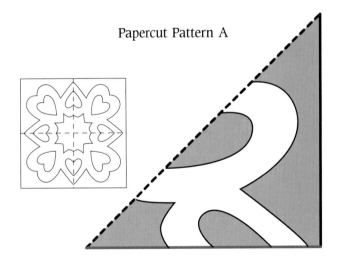

Papercut Pattern A

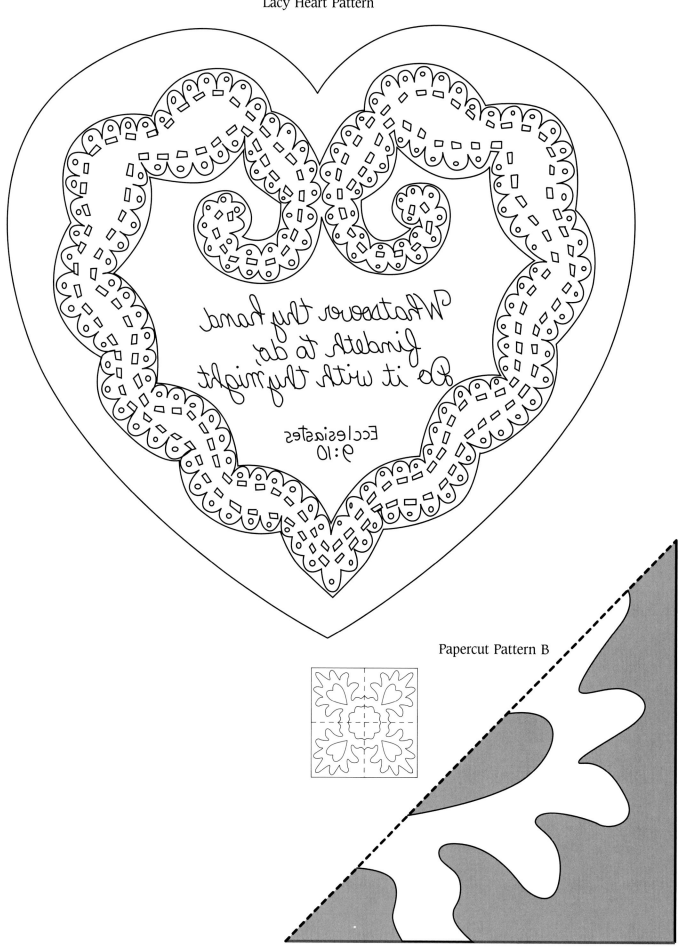

Whatsoever thy hand
findeth to do,
do it with thy might

Ecclesiastes
9:10

Papercut Pattern B

66

DARLING BASKETS

BASKET QUILT

BLOCK SIZE: 9" x 9"
QUILT SIZE: 64" x 77"

YARDAGE REQUIREMENTS
Yardage is based on 45"w fabric.

☐ 2½ yards of ecru solid
▨ 2⅜ yards of blue print
■ 1⅝ yards of blue dot
5 yards for backing
¾ yard for binding
72" x 90" batting

CUTTING OUT THE PIECES
All measurements include a ¼" seam allowance. Use patterns, pages 69-70, and follow **Template Cutting***, page 112, to cut fabric.*

1. From ecru solid: ☐
   - Cut 180 A's.
   - Cut 60 B's.
   - Cut 30 D's.
   - Cut 30 F's.

2. From blue dot: ■
   - Cut 270 A's.
   - Cut 30 C's.
   - Cut 30 E's. *(Note: Pattern for appliqué template E does not include seam allowance; add seam allowance when pieces are cut out.)*

3. From blue print: ▨
   - Cut 2 top/bottom borders 3¾" x 65".
   - Cut 6 long sashing strips 3¾" x 70¾".
   - Cut 7 strips 3¾" wide. From these strips, cut 25 short sashing strips 3¾" x 9½".

ASSEMBLING THE QUILT TOP
Follow **Piecing and Pressing***, page 112, to make quilt top.*

1. Sew 3 blue A's, 2 ecru A's, and 1 B together to make Unit 1. Make 30 Unit 1's.

Unit 1 (make 30)

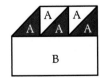

2. Sew 1 ecru A, 1 C, and 1 D together to make Unit 2. Make 30 Unit 2's.

Unit 2 (make 30)

3. Sew 1 Unit 1 and 1 Unit 2 together to make Unit 3. Make 30 Unit 3's.

Unit 3 (make 30)

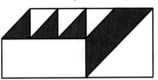

4. Sew 6 blue A's, 3 ecru A's, and 1 B together to make Unit 4. Make 30 Unit 4's.

Unit 4 (make 30)

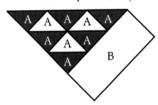

5. Sew 1 Unit 3 to 1 Unit 4 to make Unit 5. Make 30 Unit 5's.

Unit 5 (make 30)

6. Follow **Hand Appliqué**, page 116, to stitch 1 **E** to 1 **F** to make **Unit 6**. Make 30 **Unit 6's**.

Unit 6 (make 30)

7. Sew 1 **Unit 5** to 1 **Unit 6** to complete **Block**. Make 30 **Blocks**.

Block (make 30)

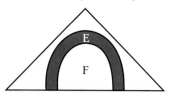

8. Sew 5 **short sashing strips** and 6 **Blocks** together to make **Row**. Make 5 **Rows**.

Row (make 5)

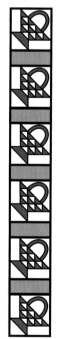

9. Sew 5 **Rows** and 6 **long sashing strips** together to make **Unit 7**.

Unit 7

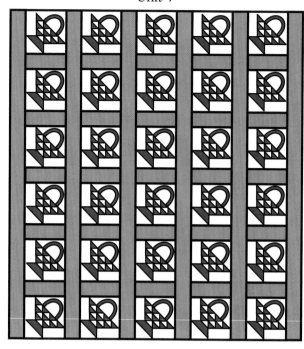

10. Sew **top/bottom borders** and **Unit 7** together to complete **Quilt Top**.

COMPLETING THE QUILT

1. Follow **Quilting**, page 117, to mark, layer, and quilt, using **Quilting Diagram** as a suggestion. Our quilt is hand quilted.
2. Cut a 27" square of binding fabric. Follow **Binding**, page 121, to bind quilt using 2½"w bias binding with mitered corners.

Quilting Diagram

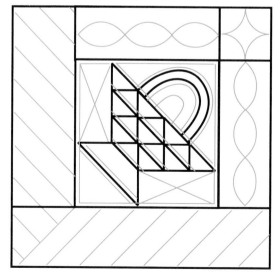

Quilt Top Diagram

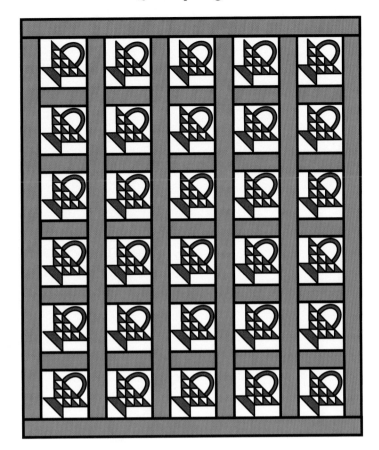

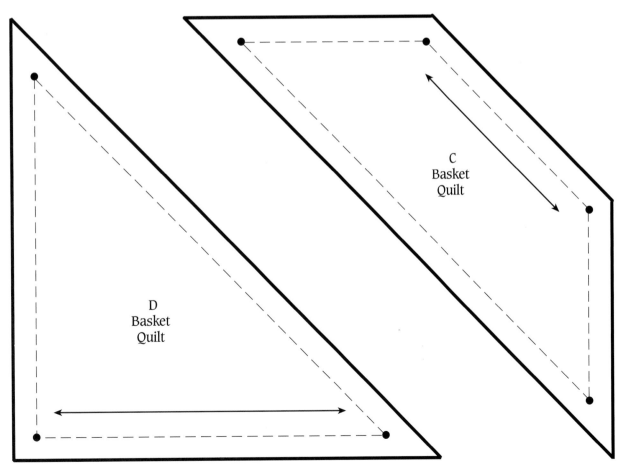

C
Basket
Quilt

D
Basket
Quilt

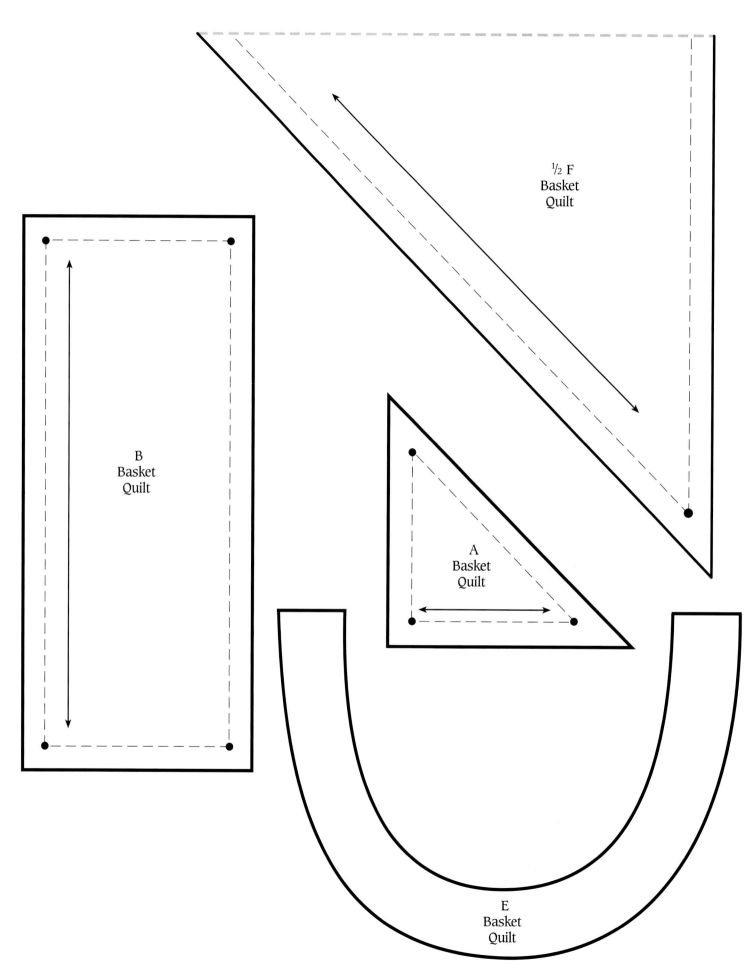

½ F
Basket
Quilt

B
Basket
Quilt

A
Basket
Quilt

E
Basket
Quilt

70

A WORLD OF FLOWERS

TRIP AROUND THE WORLD QUILT

QUILT SIZE: 78" x 93"

YARDAGE REQUIREMENTS
Yardage is based on 45"w fabric.

☐ 4 yards of white solid

◼ 1⅝ yards of pink solid

◩ ⅝ yard **each** of light blue print, light blue solid, light yellow print, light yellow solid, purple print, purple solid, and light green print

◩ ⅜ yard **each** of light green solid, orange print, orange solid, blue print, blue solid, pink print, green print, green solid, yellow print, and yellow solid

◩ ⅛ yard **each** of dark purple print and dark purple solid

5⅝ yards for backing

1 yard for binding

90" x 108" batting

You will also need:
pink embroidery floss

CUTTING OUT THE PIECES
All measurements include a ¼" seam allowance. Follow Rotary Cutting, page 110, to cut fabric.

1. From white solid: ☐
    *   Cut 56 selvage-to-selvage **strips** 2¼"w.

2. From pink solid: ◼
    *   Cut 20 selvage-to-selvage **strips** 2¼"w. From 1 strip, cut 4 **squares** 2¼" x 2¼".

3. From light blue print, light blue solid, light yellow print, light yellow solid, purple print, and purple solid: ◩
    *   Cut 8 selvage-to-selvage **strips** 2¼"w from *each* fabric.

4. From light green print: ◻
    *   Cut 6 selvage-to-selvage **strips** 2¼"w. From 1 strip, cut 4 **squares** 2¼" x 2¼".

5. From light green solid, orange print, orange solid, blue print, and blue solid: ◩
    *   Cut 5 selvage-to-selvage **strips** 2¼"w from *each* fabric.

6. From pink print: ◻
    *   Cut 4 selvage-to-selvage **strips** 2¼"w. From 1 strip, cut 4 **squares** 2¼" x 2¼".

7. From green print, green solid, yellow print, and yellow solid: ◩
    *   Cut 3 selvage-to-selvage **strips** 2¼"w from *each* fabric.

8. From dark purple print: ◼
    *   Cut 1 selvage-to-selvage strip 2¼"w. From this strip, cut 2 **squares** 2¼" x 2¼". Cut remainder of strip in half to make 2 **strips** 2¼" x 18".

9. From dark purple solid: ◼
    *   Cut 1 **strip** 2¼" x 18".

ASSEMBLING THE QUILT TOP
Follow Piecing and Pressing, page 112, to make quilt top.

1. Assemble 2¼" x 18" **strips** to make 1 **Strip Set A**. Cut across **Strip Set A** at 2¼" intervals to make 7 **Unit 1's**.

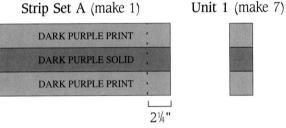

Strip Set A (make 1)   Unit 1 (make 7)

2. Assemble **strips** to make **Strip Set B**. Make 3 **Strip Set B's**. Cut across **Strip Set B's** at 2¼" intervals to make 48 **Unit 2's**.

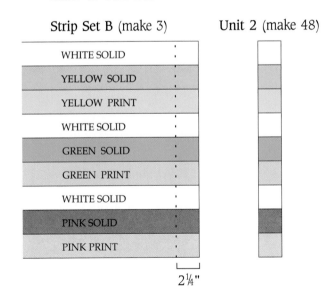

Strip Set B (make 3)   Unit 2 (make 48)

3. Assemble **strips** to make **Strip Set C**. Make 5 **Strip Set C's**. Cut across **Strip Set C's** at 2¼" intervals to make 84 **Unit 3's**.

Strip Set C (make 5)   **Unit 3 (make 84)**

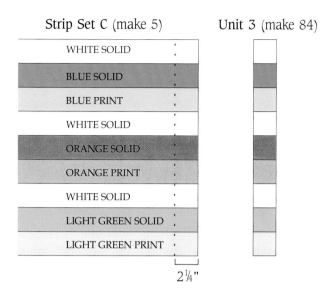

| WHITE SOLID |
| BLUE SOLID |
| BLUE PRINT |
| WHITE SOLID |
| ORANGE SOLID |
| ORANGE PRINT |
| WHITE SOLID |
| LIGHT GREEN SOLID |
| LIGHT GREEN PRINT |

2¼"

4. Assemble **strips** to make **Strip Set D**. Make 8 **Strip Set D's**. Cut across **Strip Set D** at 2¼" intervals to make 132 **Unit 4's**.

Strip Set D (make 8)   **Unit 4 (make 132)**

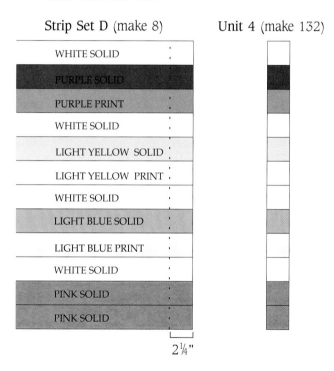

| WHITE SOLID |
| PURPLE SOLID |
| PURPLE PRINT |
| WHITE SOLID |
| LIGHT YELLOW SOLID |
| LIGHT YELLOW PRINT |
| WHITE SOLID |
| LIGHT BLUE SOLID |
| LIGHT BLUE PRINT |
| WHITE SOLID |
| PINK SOLID |
| PINK SOLID |

2¼"

5. To assemble quilt top, refer to **Assembly Diagram**, page 74, and follow Steps 5 - 8. Quilt top will be assembled in diagonal rows running from upper right to lower left. Symbols placed in the squares of the **Diagram** will help you determine where one Unit ends and another begins. For correct color sequence to develop, some Partial Units will be used. To make a Partial Unit, use a seam ripper to remove unneeded squares from a Unit.

6. Begin assembly by choosing any one of the longer diagonal rows in the **Diagram**. Arrange **Units, Partial Units,** and **squares** as indicated to make up row. Sew pieces together along short edges to complete row. Carefully check sewn row to make sure that the correct number of squares are present and colors are in the correct order. All other rows will be based on this first row.

7. Referring to **Diagram**, choose the diagonal row directly above your first sewn row. Repeat Step 6 to sew pieces together to make row. Sew the two completed rows together.

8. Moving up one row at a time, continue to arrange and sew pieces into rows, then sew rows together until top left half of quilt top is complete. Repeat to complete lower right half of quilt top.

9. To trim outer edges of quilt top, align ¼" marking on ruler (shown in yellow) with outer seam intersections as shown in **Fig. 1** and trim off excess. Machine stitch ⅛" from cut edge to prevent bias edge from stretching.

Fig. 1

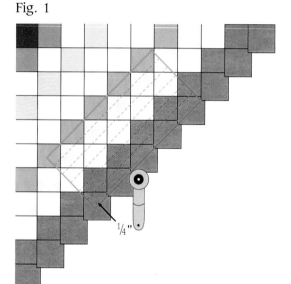

¼"

10. Referring to photo, use 3 strands of floss to work **Blanket Stitch**, page 124, around outer edges of outer row of white squares.

72

COMPLETING THE QUILT

1. Follow **Quilting**, page 117, to mark, layer, and quilt. Our quilt is hand quilted in a diagonal grid (see photo).

2. Cut a 32" square of binding fabric. Follow **Binding**, page 121, to bind quilt using 2½"w bias binding with mitered corners.

Quilt Top Diagram

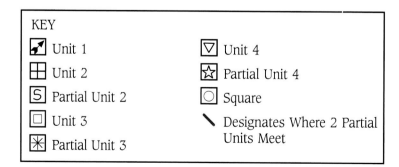

KEY

⬚ Unit 1   ▽ Unit 4

⊞ Unit 2   ☆ Partial Unit 4

S Partial Unit 2   ○ Square

□ Unit 3   ＼ Designates Where 2 Partial Units Meet

✳ Partial Unit 3

TRIP AROUND THE WORLD LAP QUILT

LAP QUILT SIZE: 52" x 67"

YARDAGE REQUIREMENTS

Yardage is based on 45"w fabric.

- [ ] 1⅜ yards of white print
- [ ] 1⅜ yards of pink print
- [ ] ⅝ yard of large blue print
- [ ] ½ yard of small blue print
- [ ] ½ yard of large purple print
- [ ] ⅜ yard of small green print
- [ ] ⅜ yard of large green print
- [ ] ⅛ yard of small purple print
  3⅝ yards for backing
  ¾ yard for binding
  72" x 90" batting

You will also need:
  pink embroidery floss

CUTTING OUT THE PIECES

All measurements include a ¼" seam allowance. Follow Rotary Cutting, page 110, to cut fabric.

1. From white print: ☐
   - Cut 13 selvage-to-selvage strips 3¼"w. From 1 strip, cut 8 squares 3¼" x 3¼".

2. From pink print: ▨
   - Cut 13 selvage-to-selvage strips 3¼"w. From 1 strip, cut 12 squares 3¼" x 3¼".

3. From large blue print: ☐
   - Cut 5 selvage-to-selvage strips 3¼"w. From 1 strip, cut 4 squares 3¼" x 3¼".

4. From small blue print: ▨
   - Cut 4 selvage-to-selvage strips 3¼"w.

5. From large purple print: ▨
   - Cut 4 selvage-to-selvage strips 3¼"w. From 1 strip, cut 4 squares 3¼" x 3¼".

6. From small green print: ▨
   - Cut 3 selvage-to-selvage strips 3¼"w.

7. From large green print: ☐
   - Cut 3 selvage-to-selvage strips 3¼"w.

8. From small purple print: ▨
   - Cut 5 squares 3¼" x 3¼".

ASSEMBLING THE QUILT TOP

Follow Piecing and Pressing, page 112, to make quilt top.

1. Assemble **strips** to make 1 **Strip Set A**. Cut across Strip Set A at 3¼" intervals to make 12 **Unit 1**'s.

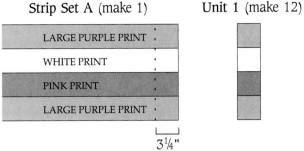

Strip Set A (make 1) Unit 1 (make 12)

2. Assemble **strips** to make 1 **Strip Set B**. Cut across Strip Set B at 3¼" intervals to make 8 **Unit 2**'s.

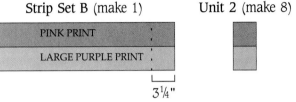

Strip Set B (make 1) Unit 2 (make 8)

3. Assemble **strips** to make **Strip Set C**. Make 3 **Strip Set C**'s. Cut across **Strip Set C**'s at 3¼" intervals to make 36 **Unit 3**'s.

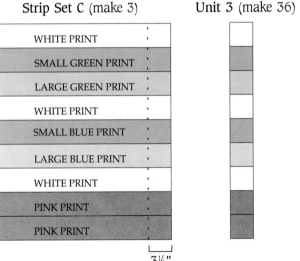

Strip Set C (make 3) Unit 3 (make 36)

4. Assemble **strips** to make 1 **Strip Set D**. Cut across Strip Set D at 3¼" intervals to make 8 **Unit 4**'s.

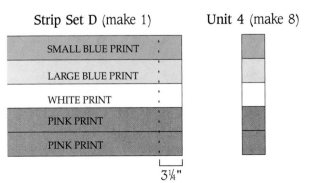

Strip Set D (make 1) Unit 4 (make 8)

75

5. Assemble **strips** to make 1 **Strip Set E**. Cut across Strip Set E at 3¼" intervals to make 8 **Unit 5's**.

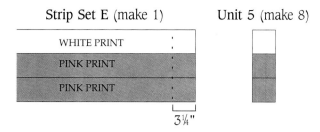

Strip Set E (make 1)

| WHITE PRINT |
| PINK PRINT |
| PINK PRINT |

Unit 5 (make 8)

3¼"

6. Referring to **Assembly Diagram** on this page, follow Steps 5 - 10 of **Assembling the Quilt Top** for **Trip Around the World Quilt**, page 72, to assemble pieces, trim edges, and add embroidery to complete **Quilt Top**.

COMPLETING THE QUILT
1. Follow **Quilting**, page 117, to mark, layer, and quilt. Our quilt is hand quilted in a grid pattern (see photo).
2. Cut a 27" square of binding fabric. Follow **Binding**, page 121, to bind quilt using 2½"w bias binding with mitered corners.

Lap Quilt Top Diagram

Assembly Diagram

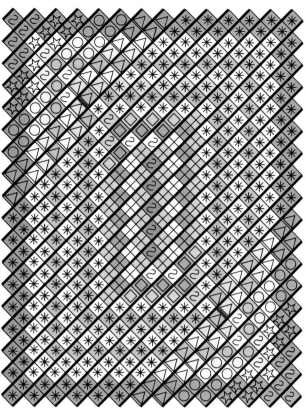

KEY	
⊞	Unit 1
☐	Unit 2
✳	Unit 3
△	Partial Unit 3
◯	Unit 4
☆	Unit 5
2	Square
╲	Designates Where 2 Partial Units Meet

TRIP AROUND THE WORLD LAP QUILT

LAP QUILT SIZE: 52" x 67"

YARDAGE REQUIREMENTS
Yardage is based on 45"w fabric.

- ☐ 1⅜ yards of white print
- ▨ 1⅜ yards of pink print
- ☐ ⅝ yard of large blue print
- ▨ ½ yard of small blue print
- ▨ ½ yard of large purple print
- ▨ ⅜ yard of small green print
- ☐ ⅜ yard of large green print
- ▨ ⅛ yard of small purple print
  3⅝ yards for backing
  ¾ yard for binding
  72" x 90" batting

You will also need:
   pink embroidery floss

CUTTING OUT THE PIECES
All measurements include a ¼" seam allowance. Follow Rotary Cutting, page 110, to cut fabric.

1. From white print: ☐
   - Cut 13 selvage-to-selvage strips 3¼"w. From 1 strip, cut 8 squares 3¼" x 3¼".

2. From pink print: ▨
   - Cut 13 selvage-to-selvage strips 3¼"w. From 1 strip, cut 12 squares 3¼" x 3¼".

3. From large blue print: ☐
   - Cut 5 selvage-to-selvage strips 3¼"w. From 1 strip, cut 4 squares 3¼" x 3¼".

4. From small blue print: ▨
   - Cut 4 selvage-to-selvage strips 3¼"w.

5. From large purple print: ▨
   - Cut 4 selvage-to-selvage strips 3¼"w. From 1 strip, cut 4 squares 3¼" x 3¼".

6. From small green print: ▨
   - Cut 3 selvage-to-selvage strips 3¼"w.

7. From large green print: ☐
   - Cut 3 selvage-to-selvage strips 3¼"w.

8. From small purple print: ▨
   - Cut 5 squares 3¼" x 3¼".

ASSEMBLING THE QUILT TOP
Follow Piecing and Pressing, page 112, to make quilt top.

1. Assemble **strips** to make 1 **Strip Set A**. Cut across **Strip Set A** at 3¼" intervals to make 12 **Unit 1's**.

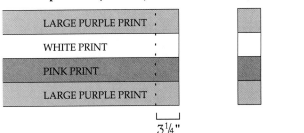

Strip Set A (make 1)
LARGE PURPLE PRINT
WHITE PRINT
PINK PRINT
LARGE PURPLE PRINT
3¼"

Unit 1 (make 12)

2. Assemble **strips** to make 1 **Strip Set B**. Cut across **Strip Set B** at 3¼" intervals to make 8 **Unit 2's**.

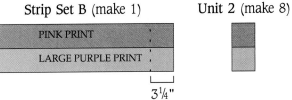

Strip Set B (make 1)
PINK PRINT
LARGE PURPLE PRINT
3¼"

Unit 2 (make 8)

3. Assemble **strips** to make **Strip Set C**. Make 3 **Strip Set C's**. Cut across **Strip Set C's** at 3¼" intervals to make 36 **Unit 3's**.

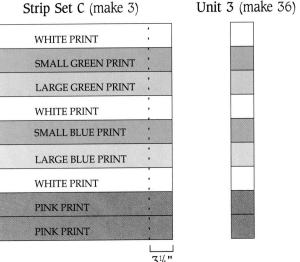

Strip Set C (make 3)
WHITE PRINT
SMALL GREEN PRINT
LARGE GREEN PRINT
WHITE PRINT
SMALL BLUE PRINT
LARGE BLUE PRINT
WHITE PRINT
PINK PRINT
PINK PRINT
3¼"

Unit 3 (make 36)

4. Assemble **strips** to make 1 **Strip Set D**. Cut across **Strip Set D** at 3¼" intervals to make 8 **Unit 4's**.

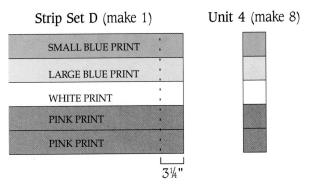

Strip Set D (make 1)
SMALL BLUE PRINT
LARGE BLUE PRINT
WHITE PRINT
PINK PRINT
PINK PRINT
3¼"

Unit 4 (make 8)

5. Assemble **strips** to make 1 **Strip Set E**. Cut across **Strip Set E** at 3¼" intervals to make 8 **Unit 5's**.

Strip Set E (make 1)   Unit 5 (make 8)

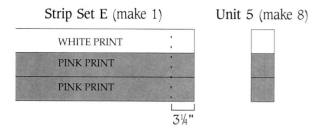

6. Referring to **Assembly Diagram** on this page, follow Steps 5 - 10 of **Assembling the Quilt Top** for **Trip Around the World Quilt**, page 72, to assemble pieces, trim edges, and add embroidery to complete Quilt Top.

COMPLETING THE QUILT

1. Follow **Quilting**, page 117, to mark, layer, and quilt. Our quilt is hand quilted in a grid pattern (see photo).
2. Cut a 27" square of binding fabric. Follow **Binding**, page 121, to bind quilt using 2½"w bias binding with mitered corners.

Lap Quilt Top Diagram

Assembly Diagram

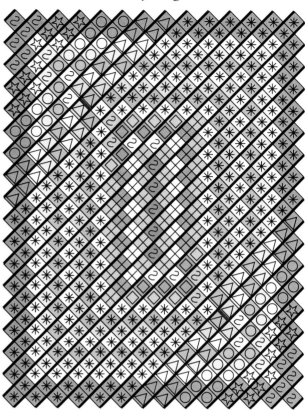

KEY	
⊞	Unit 1
☐	Unit 2
✳	Unit 3
△	Partial Unit 3
◯	Unit 4
☆	Unit 5
⊇	Square
＼	Designates Where 2 Partial Units Meet

COUNTRY FAVORITE

ROSE OF SHARON QUILT

BLOCK SIZE: 16½" x 16½"
QUILT SIZE: 66" x 82½"

YARDAGE REQUIREMENTS
Yardage is based on 45"w fabric.

☐ 5⅝ yards of cream solid

■ 1½ yards of dark pink solid

■ 1 yard of light pink solid

■ 1½ yards of green solid
5¼ yards for backing
1 yard for binding
81" x 96" batting

CUTTING OUT THE PIECES
All measurements include a ¼" seam allowance. Follow Rotary Cutting, page 110, to cut fabric.

1. From cream solid: ☐
   - Cut 2 side borders 8½" x 82".
   - Cut 2 top/bottom borders 8½" x 50".
   - Cut 12 squares 18" x 18".

PREPARING THE APPLIQUÉS
Use patterns, pages 79-80, and follow Hand Appliqué, page 116, to make appliqués.

1. From dark pink solid: ■
   - Cut 40 small roses.
   - Cut 12 medium roses.
   - Cut 48 rosebuds.

2. From light pink solid: ■
   - Cut 12 large roses.

3. From green solid: ■
   - Cut 96 A's.
   - Cut 96 B's.
   - Cut 48 C's.
   - Cut 48 stems.
   - Cut 28 vines.

ASSEMBLING THE QUILT TOP
Follow Piecing and Pressing, page 112, and Hand Appliqué, page 116, to make quilt top.

1. Referring to Block Diagram and overlapping pieces as necessary, arrange appliqués on each **square** and stitch in place. Trim square to measure 17" x 17" to complete **Block**. Make 12 **Blocks**.

2. Sew 3 **Blocks** together to make **Row**. Make 4 **Rows**.
3. Referring to **Quilt Top Diagram**, page 78, sew **Rows** together to make center section of quilt top.
4. Set aside 4 **vines** which will be appliquéd over remaining corner seams after border is attached to center section of quilt top. Follow **Hand Appliqué**, page 116, and **Quilt Top Diagram**, page 78, to stitch remaining small roses and vines to top/bottom **borders** and **side borders**.
5. Follow **Adding Squared Borders**, page 116, and **Quilt Top Diagram** to sew **top**, **bottom**, then **side borders** to center section of **Quilt Top**. Stitch pieces set aside in Step 4 over corner border seamlines to complete **Quilt Top**.

COMPLETING THE QUILT

1. Follow **Quilting**, page 117, to mark, layer, and quilt, using **Quilting Diagram** as a suggestion. Our quilt is hand quilted.
2. Cut a 29" square of binding fabric. Follow **Binding**, page 121, to bind quilt using 2½"w bias binding with mitered corners.

Quilting Diagram

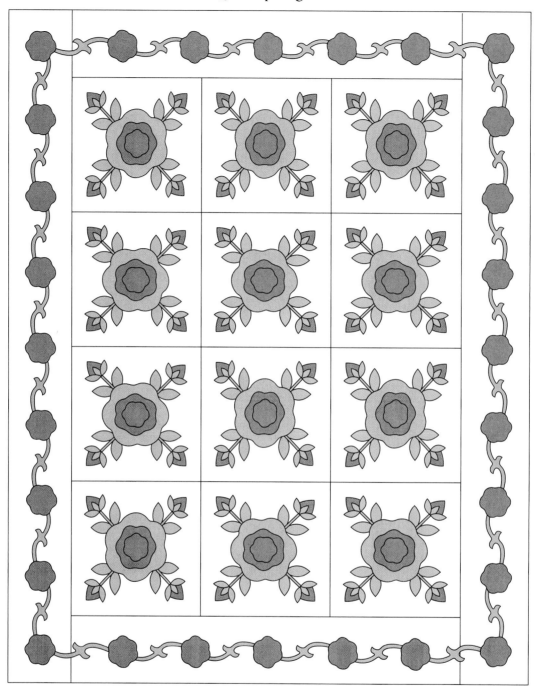

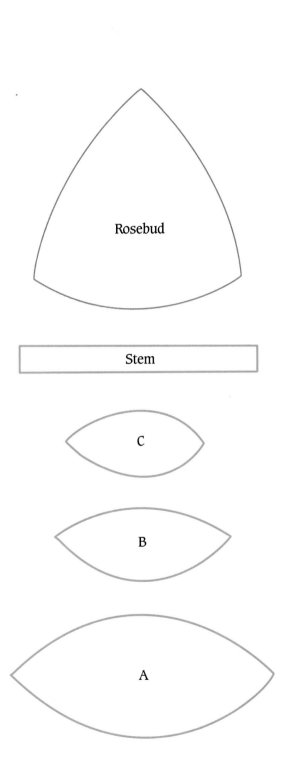

Rosebud

Stem

C

B

A

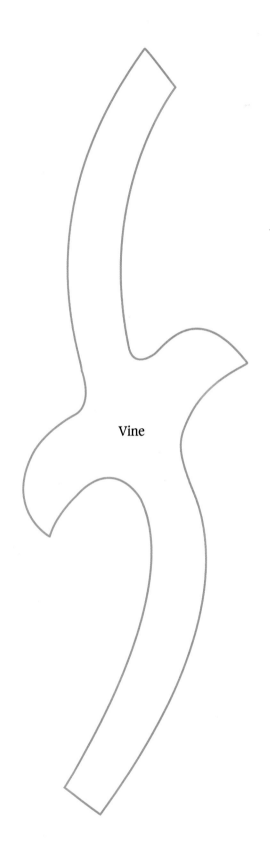

Vine

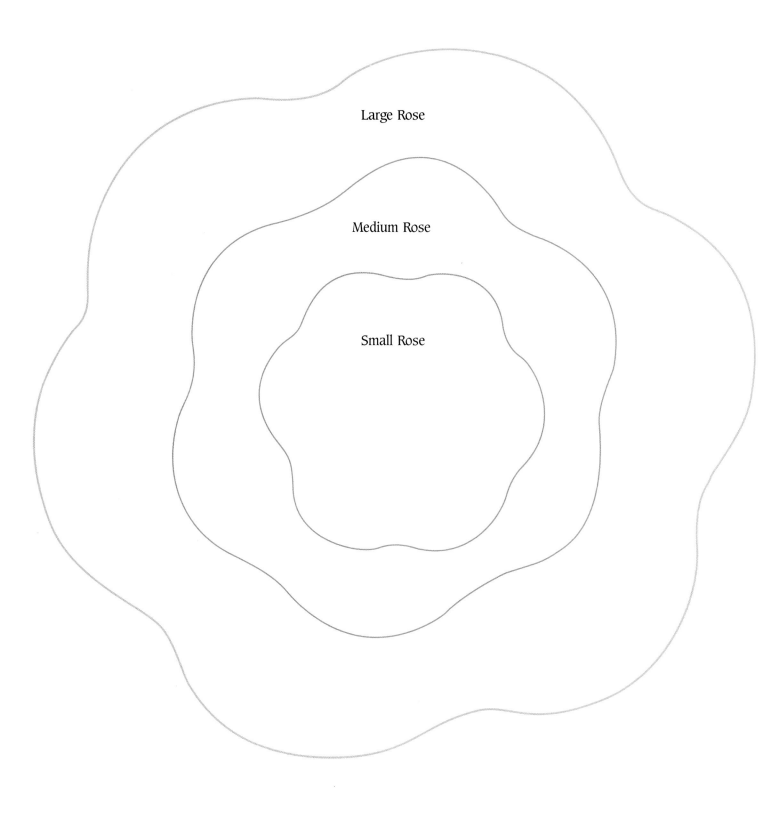

Large Rose

Medium Rose

Small Rose

WILD ROSES

WILD ROSE BOUQUET QUILT

BLOCK SIZE: 10½" x 10½"
QUILT SIZE: 84" x 99"

YARDAGE REQUIREMENTS
Yardage is based on 45"w fabric.

- [ ] 3¾ yards of white print
- 3 yards of mauve print
- 1⅝ yards of mauve/blue floral
- 1½ yards of pink print
- 1½ yards of light blue print
- 1 yard of blue
- ¾ yard of green
- ½ yard of mauve
- ¼ yard of dark mauve print
  8 yards for backing
  1 yard for binding
  90" x 108" batting

You will also need:
  paper-backed fusible web
  thread to match appliqué fabrics

CUTTING OUT THE PIECES
All measurements include a ¼" seam allowance. Follow Rotary Cutting, page 110, to cut fabric.

1. From white print: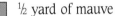
   - Cut 4 selvage-to-selvage strips 8"w. From these strips, cut a total of 20 **squares** 8" x 8".
   - Cut 1 selvage-to-selvage strip 9½"w. From this strip, cut 4 squares 9½" x 9½" for **border corner squares**.
   - Cut 2 lengthwise strips 9½" x 78½" for **side inner borders**.
   - Cut 2 lengthwise strips 9½" x 63½" for **top/bottom inner borders**.

2. From mauve print: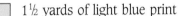
   - Cut 2 lengthwise strips 3" x 99½" for **side outer borders**.
   - Cut 2 lengthwise strips 3" x 81½" for **top/bottom outer borders**.
   - From remaining fabric width, cut 8 strips 6¼"w. From these strips, cut a total of 40 squares 6¼" x 6¼". Cut each square once diagonally to make 80 **triangles**.

square (cut 40)   triangle (cut 80)

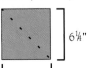

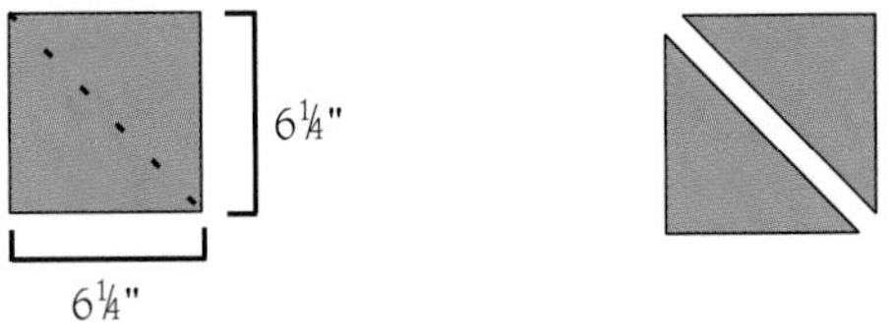

6¼"

6¼"

3. From mauve/blue floral:
   - Cut 5 selvage-to-selvage strips 6¼"w. From these strips, cut a total of 31 squares 6¼" x 6¼". Cut each square once diagonally to make 62 **triangles**.

square (cut 31)   triangle (cut 62)

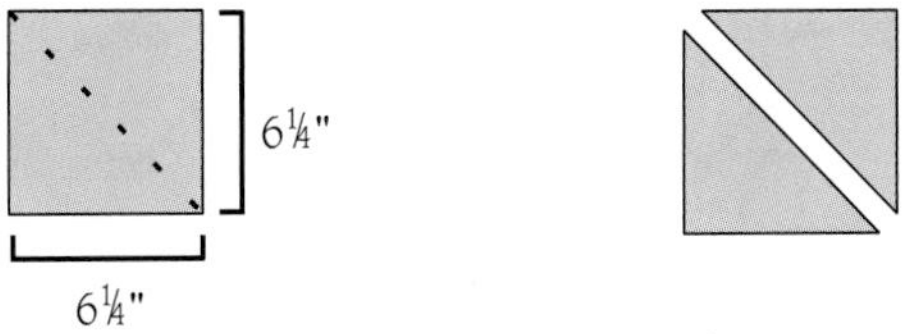

6¼"

6¼"

   - Cut 2 selvage-to-selvage strips 4⅝"w. From these strips, cut a total of 18 squares 4⅝" x 4⅝". Cut each square once diagonally to make 36 **small triangles**.

square (cut 18)   small triangle (cut 36)

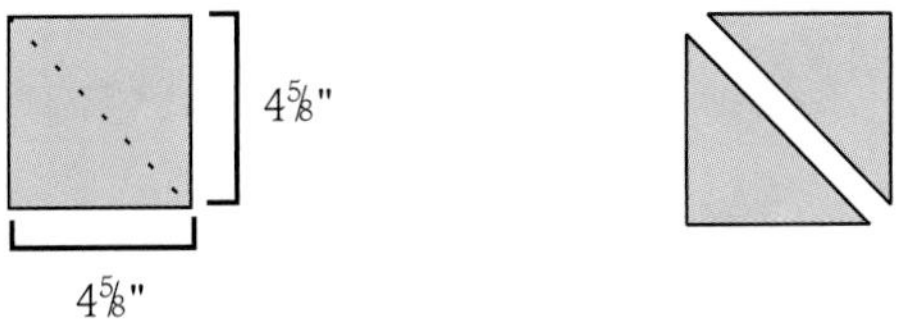

4⅝"

4⅝"

4. From pink print:
   - Cut 3 selvage-to-selvage strips 8"w. From these strips, cut a total of 12 **squares** 8" x 8".

5. From light blue print: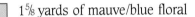
   - Cut 3 selvage-to-selvage strips 4¼"w. From these strips, cut a total of 14 **rectangles** 4¼" x 8".
   - Cut 4 squares 4¼" x 4¼".

CUTTING OUT THE APPLIQUÉS
Follow Preparing Fusible Appliqués, page 114, to cut pieces using Appliqué Patterns, pages 86 - 87.

1. From mauve/blue floral:
   - Cut 32 medium flowers.

2. From pink print:
   - Cut 32 medium flowers.
   - Cut 8 small flowers.
   - Cut 22 small flower centers.

3. From light blue print:
   - Cut 18 swags.
   - Cut 2 corner swags.
   - Cut 76 bow inner loops.
   - Cut 2 streamers (1 in reverse).

4. From blue:
   - Cut 18 swags.
   - Cut 2 corner swags.
   - Cut 38 bows.
   - Cut 2 streamers (1 in reverse).

5. From green:
   - Cut 92 leaves (46 in reverse).
   - Cut 40 pieces ⅜" x 6" for short stems.
   - Cut 20 pieces ⅜" x 7½" for long stems.
6. From mauve:
   - Cut 22 large flowers.
   - Cut 12 medium flowers.
7. From dark mauve print:
   - Cut 22 small flowers.
   - Cut 76 large flower centers.
   - Cut 8 small flower centers.

ASSEMBLING THE QUILT TOP

Follow Piecing and Pressing, page 112, to make quilt top.

1. Assemble 1 **square** and 4 **triangles** as shown to make **Block A**. Make 12 **Block A's**.

Block A (make 12)

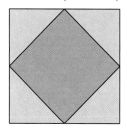

2. Assemble 1 **square** and 4 **triangles** as shown to make **Block B**. Make 20 **Block B's**.

Block B (make 20)

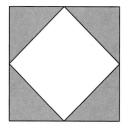

3. Follow **Satin Stitch Appliqué**, page 116, and **Quilt Top Diagram**, page 84, to appliqué **flowers**, **leaves**, **stems**, and **bows** to **Block B's**.
4. Assemble 1 **rectangle**, 2 **small triangles**, and 1 **triangle** as shown to make **Side Setting Triangle**. Make 14 **Side Setting Triangles**.

Side Setting Triangle (make 14)

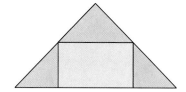

5. Assemble 1 **square** and 2 **small triangles** as shown to make **Corner Setting Triangle**. Make 4 **Corner Setting Triangles**.

Corner Setting Triangle (make 4)

6. Referring to **Assembly Diagram**, page 83, assemble **Block A's**, **Block B's**, **Side Setting Triangles**, and **Corner Setting Triangles** into rows; sew rows together to complete center section of quilt top.
7. Refer to Steps 1 and 2 of **Adding Squared Borders**, page 116, to trim **top/bottom** and **side inner borders** to fit raw edges of center section of quilt top.
8. Assemble 2 **border corner squares** and 1 **side inner border** as shown to make **Side Inner Border Unit**. Make 2 **Side Inner Border Units**.

Side Inner Border Unit (make 2)

9. Set aside 4 **small flowers**, 4 **small flower centers**, and 8 **leaves** (4 in reverse), which will be appliquéd over remaining corner seams after border is attached to center section of quilt top. Follow **Satin Stitch Appliqué**, page 116, and **Quilt Top Diagram**, page 84, to appliqué remaining **flowers**, **leaves**, **swags**, **bows**, and **streamers** to **top/bottom inner borders** and **Side Inner Border Units**.
10. Follow **Adding Squared Borders**, page 116, and **Quilt Top Diagram** to attach **top** and **bottom inner borders** and then **Side Inner Border Units** to center section of quilt top. Appliqué pieces set aside in Step 9 over corner border seamlines.
11. Add **top**, **bottom**, and then **side outer borders** to complete **Quilt Top**.

COMPLETING THE QUILT

1. Follow **Quilting**, page 117, to mark, layer, and quilt, using **Quilting Diagram**, page 83, as a suggestion. Our quilt is hand quilted.
2. Cut a 36" square of binding fabric. Follow **Binding**, page 121, to bind quilt using 2½"w bias binding with mitered corners.

Quilting Diagram

Assembly Diagram

84

NOSEGAY VALANCE

VALANCE SIZE: 13" x 47"

Our valance will fit a window approximately 38" wide.

SUPPLIES

☐ 1⅜ yards of white print fabric

▨ scraps of assorted fabrics for appliqués
paper-backed fusible web
64" long 1½"w fabric strip
thread to match appliqué fabrics

MAKING THE VALANCE

Follow Piecing and Pressing, page 112, to make valance.

1. Using patterns, pages 86 - 87, follow **Preparing Fusible Appliqués**, page 114, to make **flower, flower center, leaf, stem,** and **bow** appliqués.

2. Cut a 27" x 48" rectangle from white print fabric. Referring to **Fig. 1**, fold rectangle in half lengthwise and press to form crease. Fold in half crosswise twice and press in creases.

Fig. 1

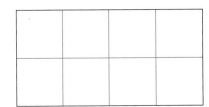

3. Referring to **Valance Diagram**, this page, and using pressed creases for reference, arrange appliqués on valance, overlapping as necessary, and fuse in place. Follow **Satin Stitch Appliqué**, page 116, to stitch around appliqués.

4. Matching wrong sides, fold fabric strip in half lengthwise; stitch ¼" from long edges, forming a tube. Centering seam along back of tube, press tube flat. Referring to **Valance Diagram**, position tube on valance, folding at corners to miter. Pin or baste in place. Follow **Hand Appliqué**, page 116, to stitch tube in place.

5. Matching right sides and raw edges, fold valance in half lengthwise. Stitch ½" from long raw edges, forming a tube; turn right side out. Fold raw edges at each end of tube ½" to inside; press. Beginning 1½" from top folded edge, topstitch close to folded edges through all layers at each end of valance (**Fig. 2**).

Fig. 2

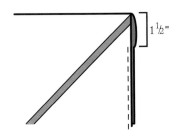

6. To form rod pocket, topstitch along top of valance 1½" from folded edge.

Valance Diagram

ROSY TABLE TOPPER

TABLE TOPPER SIZE: 45" x 45"

YARDAGE REQUIREMENTS

Yardage is based on 45"w fabric.

☐ 44" x 44" square of white print for table topper

▨ 1 fat quarter (18" x 22" piece) **each** of mauve/blue floral, pink print, dark mauve print, mauve, light blue print, blue, and green for appliqués
5 yards of 2½"w bias binding (pieced if necessary)

You will also need:
paper-backed fusible web
thread to match appliqué fabrics

CUTTING OUT THE APPLIQUÉS

Follow Preparing Fusible Appliques, page 114, to cut pieces using Appliqué Patterns, pages 86 - 87.

1. From mauve/blue floral: ▨
   - Cut 4 medium flowers.

2. From pink print: ▢
   - Cut 4 medium flowers.
   - Cut 4 small flower centers.

3. From dark mauve print: ■
   - Cut 4 small flowers.
   - Cut 8 large flower centers.

4. From mauve: ▢
   - Cut 4 large flowers.

5. From light blue print: ▢
   - Cut 8 bow inner loops.

6. From blue: ▢
   - Cut 4 bows.

7. From green: ▢
   - Cut 8 leaves (4 in reverse).
   - Cut 8 pieces ⅜" x 6" for **short stems**.
   - Cut 4 pieces ⅜" x 7½" for **long stems**.

MAKING THE TABLE TOPPER

1. Referring to photo, follow **Satin Stitch Appliqué**, page 116, to appliqué **flowers, leaves, stems,** and **bow** to each corner of table topper.

2. Follow **Attaching Binding with Mitered Corners**, page 122, to attach binding to table topper.

85

PILLOW SHAMS

PILLOW SHAM SIZE: 20" x 26"

YARDAGE REQUIREMENTS
Yardage is based on 45"w fabric.

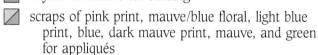

☐ 3 yards of white print

▨ ¼ yard of mauve for binding

▱ scraps of pink print, mauve/blue floral, light blue print, blue, dark mauve print, mauve, and green for appliqués

You will also need:
    paper-backed fusible web
    thread to match appliqué fabrics

CUTTING OUT THE PIECES
1. From white print: ☐
   - Cut 1 square 18" x 18". Cut once diagonally to cut 2 triangles for **flaps**.
   - Cut 2 rectangles 21" x 27" for **sham tops**.
   - Cut 4 rectangles 16½" x 21" for **sham backs**.
2. From mauve: ▨
   - Cut 2 selvage-to-selvage strips 2½"w for binding.

CUTTING OUT THE APPLIQUÉS
Follow Preparing Fusible Appliqués, page 114, to cut pieces using Appliqué Patterns, pages 86 - 87.

1. From pink print: ▨
   - Cut 2 medium flowers.
   - Cut 2 small flower centers.
2. From mauve/blue floral: ▱
   - Cut 2 medium flowers.
3. From light blue print: ☐
   - Cut 4 bow inner loops.
4. From blue: ▨
   - Cut 2 bows.
5. From dark mauve print: ■
   - Cut 2 small flowers.
   - Cut 4 large flower centers.
6. From mauve: ▨
   - Cut 2 large flowers.
7. From green: ▨
   - Cut 4 leaves (2 in reverse).
   - Cut 4 pieces ⅜" x 6" for **short stems**.
   - Cut 2 pieces ⅜" x 7½" for **long stems**.

MAKING THE SHAMS
1. Referring to photo, follow **Satin Stitch Appliqué**, page 116, to appliqué **flowers, stems, leaves,** and **bow** to each **flap**.

2. Referring to Steps 3 - 6 and 8 of **Attaching Binding with Mitered Corners**, page 122, use 2½"w **strips** to bind lower edges of each flap. Trim binding even with edge of flap at each end.
3. On each sham back piece, press one 21" edge ½" to wrong side; press ½" to wrong side again and stitch in place.
4. For each **sham back**, place 2 sham back pieces right side up. Referring to **Fig. 1**, overlap finished edges and baste in place.

Fig. 1

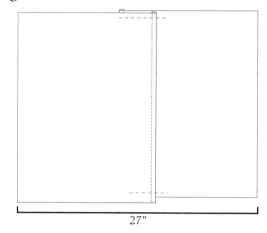

27"

5. To complete each sham, match right sides and long raw edges and center flap on sham back. Place **sham top**, wrong side up, on flap and back. Stitch through all layers ½" from raw edges. Cut corners diagonally; remove basting threads at opening. Turn sham right side out; press.

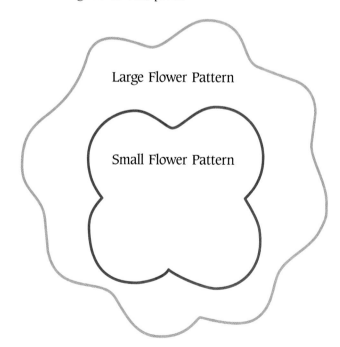

Large Flower Pattern

Small Flower Pattern

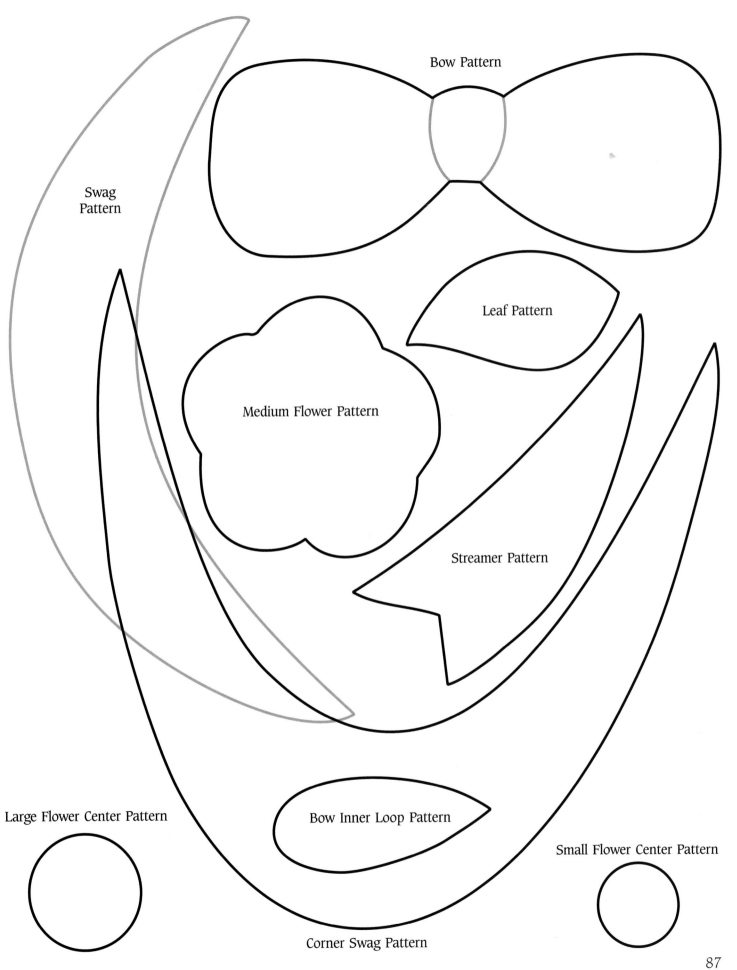

Bow Pattern

Swag
Pattern

Leaf Pattern

Medium Flower Pattern

Streamer Pattern

Large Flower Center Pattern

Bow Inner Loop Pattern

Small Flower Center Pattern

Corner Swag Pattern

DAINTY DRESDEN

DRESDEN PLATE QUILT

BLOCK SIZE: 15½" x 15½"
QUILT SIZE: 90" x 109"

YARDAGE REQUIREMENTS
Yardage is based on 45"w fabric.

- 6¼ yards of cream solid
- 3 yards of green print
- ¾ yard **each** of 2 pink prints, 2 red prints, 2 purple prints, and 1 dark green print
- ⅝ yard of purple solid
- 2 yards of organdy or other very lightweight cotton fabric
- 8¼ yards for backing
- 1 yard for binding
- 120" x 120" batting

You will also need:
  transparent monofilament thread for appliqué
  pinking shears (optional)

CUTTING OUT THE PIECES
All measurements include a ¼" seam allowance. Follow Rotary Cutting, page 110, and Template Cutting, page 112, to cut fabric.

1. From cream solid: ☐
   - Cut 2 lengthwise strips 6½" x 99" for **side borders**.
   - Cut 2 lengthwise strips 6½" x 94" for **top/bottom borders**.
   - Cut 7 strips 16"w. From these strips, cut 14 squares 16" x 16". From remaining fabric width, cut 6 squares 16" x 16" for a total of 20 background squares.

2. From green print: ▨
   - Cut 5 strips 16"w. From these strips, cut 49 sashing strips 3½" x 16".
   - Cut 40 A's using Template A pattern, page 91.

3. From *each* of the 2 pink prints, 2 red prints, 2 purple prints, and 1 dark green print: ◨
   - Cut 40 A's using Template A.

4. From purple solid: ■
   - Cut 3 strips 3½"w. From these strips, cut 30 sashing squares 3½" x 3½".
   - Cut 20 B's using Template B pattern, page 91.

5. From organdy:
   - Cut 32 strips 1½"w. From these strips, cut 320 lining rectangles 1½" x 4".
   - Cut 20 B's using Template B.

ASSEMBLING THE QUILT TOP
Follow Piecing and Pressing, page 112, to make quilt top.

1. Referring to **Fig. 1**, place 1 **lining rectangle** and 1 A right sides together. Stitch from dot to dot ¼" from curved edge of A, backstitching at beginning and end of seam. Repeat with remaining A's.

Fig. 1

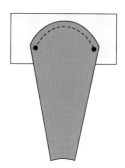

2. Referring to **Fig. 2**, trim excess lining fabric even with side edges of A; use pinking shears to trim seam allowance along curve to ⅛" (trim to ⅛" and clip curve if not using pinking shears). Repeat with remaining A's.

Fig. 2   A (make 320)

3. Referring to diagram for color placement, sew 16 A's together to make **Unit 1**. Make 20 **Unit 1's**.

Unit 1 (make 20)

4. Place 1 purple **B** and 1 organdy **B** right sides together; stitch ¼" from edge. Use pinking shears to trim seam allowance to ⅛". To make opening for turning, cut a slit in organdy only (**Fig. 3**). Turn right side out and press. Repeat with remaining **B**'s.

Fig. 3   B (make 20)

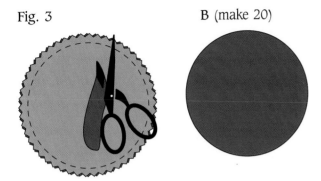

5. Center 1 **B** over hole in center of 1 **Unit 1**. Follow Mock Hand Appliqué, page 115, to stitch **B** to **Unit 1** to make **Unit 2**. Make 20 **Unit 2**'s.

Unit 2 (make 20)

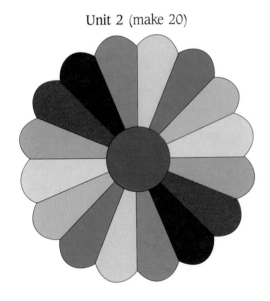

6. Fold **background square** in half twice and press folds; unfold. Using pressed lines as placement guidelines, center **Unit 2** on **background square**. Follow Mock Hand Appliqué, page 115, to stitch **Unit 2** to **background square** to complete **Block**. Make 20 **Blocks**.

Block (make 20)

7. Sew 5 **sashing strips** and 4 **Blocks** together to make **Row**. Make 5 **Rows**.

Row (make 5)

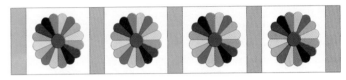

8. Sew 5 **sashing squares** and 4 **sashing strips** together to make **Sashing Row**. Make 6 **Sashing Rows**.

Sashing Row (make 6)

9. Referring to **Quilt Top Diagram**, page 90, sew **Sashing Rows** and **Rows** together to make center section of quilt top.

10. Follow Adding Squared Borders, page 116, to sew side, then **top** and **bottom borders** to center section to complete **Quilt Top**.

COMPLETING THE QUILT

1. Follow Quilting, page 117, to mark, layer, and quilt, using Quilting Diagram, page 91, as a suggestion. Our quilt is hand quilted using outline, feather, and cable designs.

2. Cut a 36" square of binding fabric. Follow Binding, page 121, to bind quilt using 2½"w bias binding with mitered corners.

Quilting Diagram

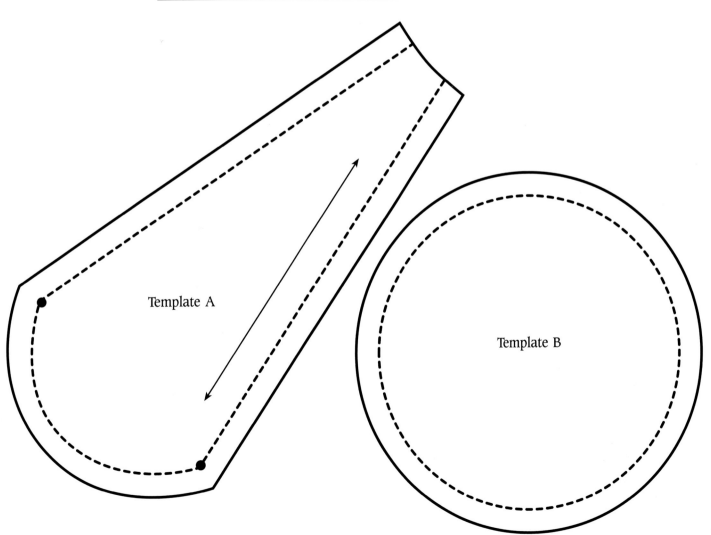

Template A

Template B

GARDEN WEDDING

GARDEN WEDDING QUILT

QUILT SIZE: 91" x 109"

YARDAGE REQUIREMENTS
Yardage is based on 45"w fabric.

☐ 6¼ yards of cream print
☐ 3¼ yards of green print
☐ 2¼ yards of pink print
☐ ¾ yard of yellow print
   8¼ yards for backing
   1 yard for binding
   120" x 120" batting

You will also need:
   paper-backed fusible web
   transparent monofilament thread for appliqué

CUTTING OUT THE PIECES
All measurements include a ¼" seam allowance. Follow Rotary Cutting, page 110, to cut fabric unless otherwise indicated.

1. From cream print: ☐
   • Cut 51 strips 2½"w.
   • Cut 6 wide strips 3¼"w.
   • Cut 5 strips 4½"w. From these strips, cut 40 squares 4½" x 4½".
   • Cut 5 strips 6½"w. From these strips, cut 25 small rectangles 2½" x 6½" and 24 large rectangles 4½" x 6½".

2. From green print: ☐
   • Cut 30 strips 2½"w.
   • Cut 3 narrow strips 1"w.
   • Cut 3 strips 4½"w. From these strips, cut 20 squares 4½" x 4½".
   • Use pattern, page 98, and follow Preparing Fusible Appliqués, page 114, to make 50 leaf appliqués.

3. From pink print: ☐
   • Cut 28 strips 2½"w.

4. From yellow print: ☐
   • Cut 8 strips 2½"w.

ASSEMBLING THE QUILT TOP
Follow Piecing and Pressing, page 112, to make quilt top.

1. Sew 3 strips together to make Strip Set A. Make 7 Strip Set A's. Cut across Strip Set A's at 2½" intervals to make 104 Unit 1's.

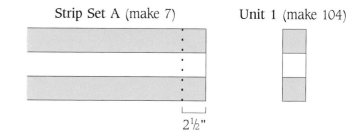

Strip Set A (make 7)   Unit 1 (make 104)

2½"

2. Sew 3 strips together to make Strip Set B. Make 3 Strip Set B's. Cut across Strip Set B's at 2½" intervals to make 34 Unit 2's.

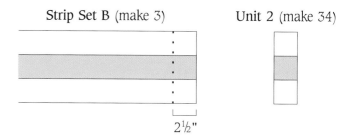

Strip Set B (make 3)   Unit 2 (make 34)

2½"

3. Sew 3 strips together to make Strip Set C. Make 7 Strip Set C's. Cut across 3 Strip Set C's at 2½" intervals to make 48 Unit 3's. Cut across 2 Strip Set C's at 4½" intervals to make 18 Unit 4's. Cut across remaining Strip Set C's at 6½" intervals to make 22 Unit 5's.

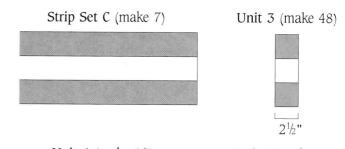

Strip Set C (make 7)   Unit 3 (make 48)

2½"

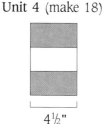

Unit 4 (make 18)

4½"

Unit 5 (make 22)

6½"

4. Sew 3 strips together to make **Strip Set D**. Make 3 Strip Set D's. Cut across **Strip Set D's** at 2½" intervals to make 48 **Unit 6's**.

Strip Set D (make 3)   Unit 6 (make 48)

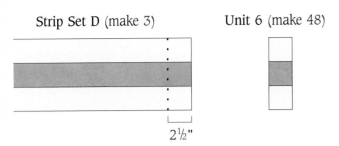

2½"

5. Sew 2 strips together to make **Strip Set E**. Make 10 Strip Set E's. Cut across **Strip Set E's** at 2½" intervals to make 160 **Unit 7's**.

Strip Set E (make 10)   Unit 7 (make 160)

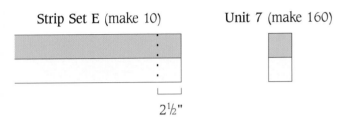

2½"

6. Sew 2 strips together to make **Strip Set F**. Make 5 Strip Set F's. Cut across **Strip Set F's** at 4½" intervals to make 40 **Unit 8's**.

Strip Set F (make 5)   Unit 8 (make 40)

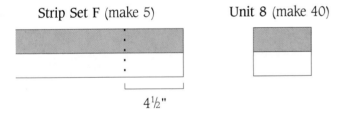

4½"

7. Sew 3 strips together to make **Strip Set G**. Make 4 Strip Set G's. Cut across **Strip Set G's** at 2½" intervals to make 50 **Unit 9's**.

Strip Set G (make 4)   Unit 9 (make 50)

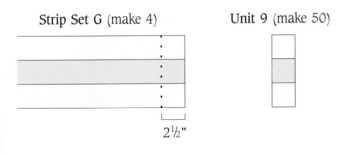

2½"

8. Sew 3 strips together to make **Strip Set H**. Make 2 Strip Set H's. Cut across **Strip Set H's** at 2½" intervals to make 25 **Unit 10's**.

Strip Set H (make 2)   Unit 10 (make 25)

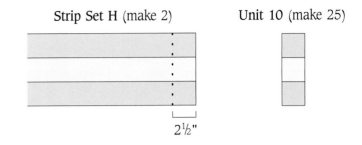

2½"

9. Sew 1 **narrow** and 2 **wide strips** together to make **Strip Set I**. Make 3 Strip Set I's. Cut across **Strip Set I's** at 4½" intervals to make 25 **Unit 11's**.

Strip Set I (make 3)   Unit 11 (make 25)

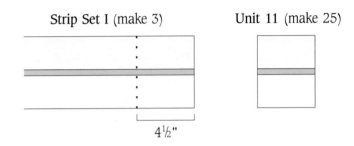

4½"

10. Sew 3 strips together to make **Strip Set J**. Make 3 Strip Set J's. Cut across **Strip Set J's** at 2½" intervals to make 36 **Unit 12's**.

Strip Set J (make 3)   Unit 12 (make 36)

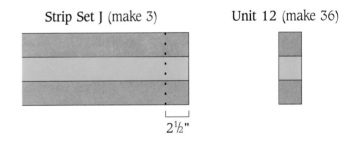

2½"

11. Sew 2 Unit 1's and 1 Unit 2 together to make Block A. Make 34 Block A's.

Block A (make 34)

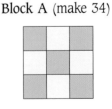

12. Sew 2 Unit 3's, 2 Unit 6's, and 1 **large rectangle** together to make **Block B**. Make 24 **Block B's**.

Block B (make 24)

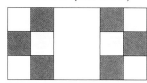

13. Sew 2 Unit 7's together to make Unit 13. Make 80 Unit 13's.

Unit 13 (make 80)

14. Sew 2 Unit 13's and 1 Unit 8 together to make Unit 14. Make 40 Unit 14's.

Unit 14 (make 40)

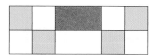

15. Sew 3 **squares** together to make Unit 15. Make 20 Unit 15's.

Unit 15 (make 20)

16. Sew 2 Unit 14's and 1 Unit 15 together to make Block C. Make 20 Block C's.

Block C (make 20)

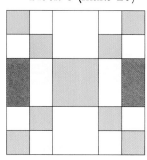

17. Sew 2 Unit 9's and 1 Unit 10 together to make Unit 16. Make 25 Unit 16's.

Unit 16 (make 25)

18. Sew 1 **small rectangle**, 1 Unit 16, and 1 Unit 11 together to make Unit 17. Make 25 Unit 17's.

Unit 17 (make 25)

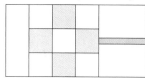

19. Follow **Invisible Appliqué**, page 115, to stitch 2 **leaf** appliqués to 1 Unit 17 to make **Block D**. Make 25 **Block D's**.

Block D (make 25)

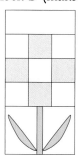

20. Sew 1 Unit 1 and 1 Unit 12 together to make Unit 18. Make 36 Unit 18's.

Unit 18 (make 36)

21. Sew 2 Unit 18's and 1 Unit 4 together to make Block E. Make 18 Block E's.

Block E (make 18)

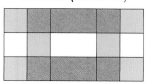

22. Sew 2 Block A's, 5 Unit 5's, and 4 Block E's together to make Row A. Make 2 Row A's.

Row A (make 2)

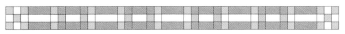

23. Sew 2 Unit 5's, 5 Block A's, and 4 Block B's together to make Row B. Make 6 Row B's.

Row B (make 6)

24. Sew 2 Block E's, 5 Block D's, and 4 Block C's together to make Row C. Make 5 Row C's.

Row C (make 5)

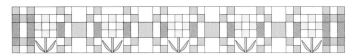

25. Referring to Quilt Top Diagram, page 95, sew Rows together to complete Quilt Top.

COMPLETING THE QUILT

1. Follow Quilting, page 117, to mark, layer, and quilt using Quilting Diagram as a suggestion. Our quilt is hand quilted.
2. Cut a 34" square of binding fabric. Follow Binding, page 121, to bind quilt using 2½"w bias binding with mitered corners.

Quilting Diagram

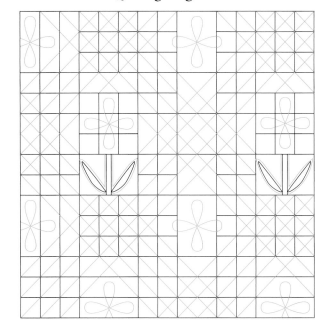

WEDDING DAY WALL HANGING

WALL HANGING SIZE: 22" x 22"

YARDAGE REQUIREMENTS
Yardage is based on 45"w fabric.

☐ ½ yard of green print
☐ ⅜ yard of cream print
☐ ⅛ yard of pink print
☐ ⅛ yard of yellow solid
◺ scraps of assorted prints for appliqués
   ¾ yard for backing and hanging sleeve
   ⅜ yard for binding
   25" x 25" batting

You will also need:
   paper-backed fusible web
   transparent monofilament thread for appliqué
   black permanent fabric pen

CUTTING OUT THE PIECES
All measurements include a ¼" seam allowance. Follow Rotary Cutting, page 110, to cut fabric unless otherwise indicated.

1. From green print: ☐
   • Cut 1 background 16" x 16".
   • Cut 8 squares 2⅝" x 2⅝".

2. From cream print: ☐
   • Cut 2 strips 4¼"w. From these strips, cut 12 squares 4¼" x 4¼". Cut squares twice diagonally to make 48 triangles.

3. From pink print: ☐
   • Cut 1 strip 2⅝"w. From this strip, cut 8 squares 2⅝" x 2⅝".

4. From yellow solid: ☐
   • Cut 1 strip 2⅝"w. From this strip, cut 8 squares 2⅝" x 2⅝".

5. From remaining fabric and scraps: ◺
   • Referring to photo, use patterns, page 98, and follow Preparing Fusible Appliqués, page 114, to make the following appliqués:
     2 hands (1 in reverse)   3 flowers
     3 hearts   3 flower centers
     2 rings   3 small leaves

ASSEMBLING THE WALL HANGING TOP

Refer to photo and Wall Hanging Top Diagram and follow Piecing and Pressing, page 112, to make wall hanging top.

1. Use permanent fabric pen to write words on **rings**.
2. Follow **Invisible Appliqué**, page 115, to stitch **pieces** to **background**. Trim **background** to measure 15½" x 15½".
3. Use **triangles** and **squares** to make 4 Unit 1's, 8 Unit 2's, 8 Unit 3's, and 4 Unit 4's.

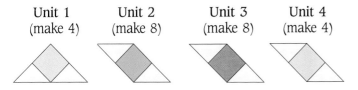

| Unit 1 (make 4) | Unit 2 (make 8) | Unit 3 (make 8) | Unit 4 (make 4) |

4. Sew 1 **Unit 1**, 2 **Unit 2's**, 2 **Unit 3's**, and 1 **Unit 4** together to make **Border Unit**. Make 4 **Border Units**.

Border Unit (make 4)

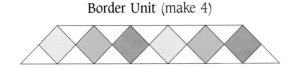

5. Beginning and ending stitching exactly ¼" from each corner of background and backstitching at beginning and end of each seam, sew 1 **Border Unit** to each edge of **background**.
6. Fold 1 corner of wall hanging top diagonally with right sides together, matching outer edges of borders. Beginning at point where previous seams end, stitch corner seam (**Fig. 1**) to complete **Wall Hanging Top**.

Fig. 1

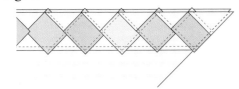

COMPLETING THE WALL HANGING

1. Follow **Quilting**, page 117, to mark, layer, and quilt using **Quilting Diagram** as a suggestion. Our wall hanging is hand quilted.
2. Follow **Making a Hanging Sleeve**, page 123, to attach hanging sleeve.
3. Follow **Binding**, page 121, to bind quilt using 2½"w straight-grain binding with overlapped corners.

Wall Hanging Top Diagram

Quilting Diagram

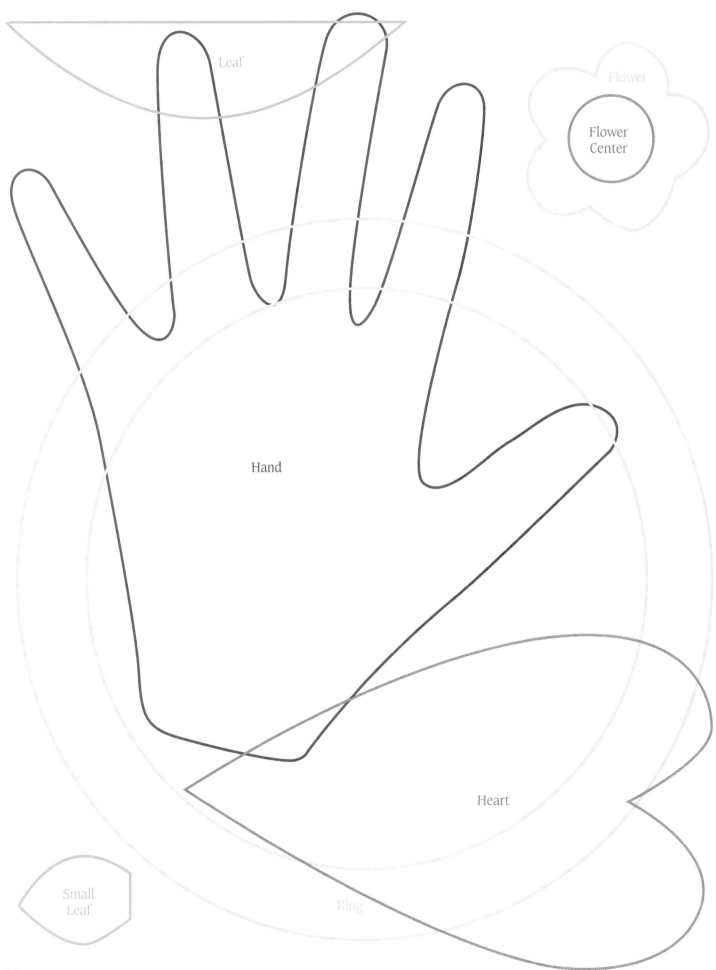

Leaf

Flower

Flower
Center

Hand

Heart

Small
Leaf

Ring

SPRINGTIME FLOWER BASKETS

TULIP BASKET QUILT

BLOCK SIZE: 14" x 14"
QUILT SIZE: 75" x 94"

YARDAGE REQUIREMENTS
Yardage is based on 45"w fabric.

- ☐ 8 yards of white solid
- ☐ 1 yard of green solid
- ☐ ¾ yard of blue solid
- ☐ ¾ yard of pink solid
- ☐ ½ yard of yellow solid
- ☐ ½ yard of purple solid
- 5¾ yards for backing
- 1 yard for binding
- 90" x 108" batting

You will also need:
¼"w bias pressing bar

CUTTING OUT THE PIECES
All measurements include a ¼" seam allowance. Follow Rotary Cutting, page 110, to cut fabric.

1. From white solid: ☐
   - Cut 2 lengthwise **side borders** 7½" x 98½".
   - Cut 2 lengthwise **top/bottom borders** 7½" x 81".
   - Cut 3 strips 14½" wide. From these strips, cut 6 **setting squares** 14½" x 14½".
   - Cut 6 strips 15½" wide. From these strips, cut 12 **background squares** 15½" x 15½".
   - Cut 3 squares 21" x 21". Cut squares twice diagonally to make 12 **side triangles**. (You will need 10 and have 2 left over.)
   - Cut 2 squares 10¾" x 10¾". Cut squares once diagonally to make 4 **corner triangles**.

2. From green solid: ☐
   - Cut 1 **square** 12" x 12" for bias strip.

PREPARING THE APPLIQUÉS
Use patterns, pages 100-102, and follow Template Cutting, page 112, to make appliqués.

1. From blue solid: ☐
   - Cut 12 **baskets**.
   - Cut 24 **handles** (12 in reverse).

2. From green solid: ☐
   - Cut 10 **vines**.
   - Cut 20 **leaf A's** (10 in reverse).
   - Cut 20 **leaf B's** (10 in reverse).
   - Cut 24 **leaf C's** (12 in reverse).
   - Cut 24 **leaf D's** (12 in reverse).

3. From pink, yellow, and purple solids for flower appliqués: ◪
   - Cut 32 **tulips** from pink solid.
   - Cut 32 **petals** from pink solid.
   - Cut 18 **tulips** from yellow solid.
   - Cut 18 **petals** from yellow solid.
   - Cut 18 **tulips** from purple solid.
   - Cut 18 **petals** from purple solid.

ASSEMBLING THE QUILT TOP
Follow Piecing and Pressing, page 112, and Hand Appliqué, page 116, to make quilt top.

1. To make bias tube for **stems**, use square and follow Steps 1-6 of **Making Continuous Bias Strip Binding**, page 121, to make 1½"w continuous bias strip.
2. Fold bias strip in half lengthwise with wrong sides together; do not press. Stitch ¼" from long raw edges to form tube; trim seam allowance to ⅛". Place bias pressing bar inside one end of tube. Center seam at back of bar and press as you move bar down length of tube. Cut tube into desired lengths for **stems**.
3. Referring to **Block Diagram** and overlapping pieces as necessary, arrange appliqués and stem pieces on background square; stitch in place. Trim square to 14½" x 14½" to complete **Block**. Make 12 **Blocks**.

Block Diagram

4. Referring to **Quilt Top Diagram**, page 101, and overlapping pieces as necessary, arrange appliqués on **top**, **bottom**, and **side borders** and stitch in place.
5. Referring to **Assembly Diagram**, page 100, sew corner triangles, side triangles, Blocks and setting squares together to make center section of quilt top.
6. Referring to **Quilt Top Diagram**, page 101, follow **Adding Mitered Borders**, page 117, to add borders to complete **Quilt Top**.

COMPLETING THE QUILT
1. Follow **Quilting**, page 117, to mark, layer, and quilt, using **Quilting Diagram**, page 101, as a suggestion. Our quilt is hand quilted.
2. Cut a 29" square of binding fabric. Follow **Binding**, page 121, to bind quilt using 2½"w bias binding with mitered corners.

Assembly Diagram

Tulip

Petal

Quilt Top Diagram

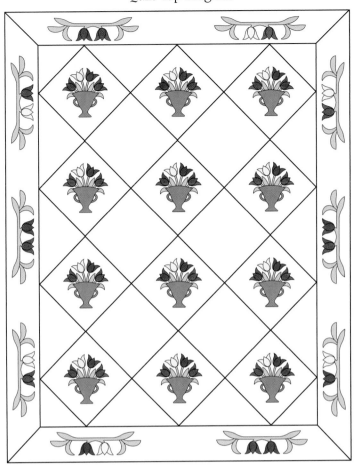

Quilting Diagram

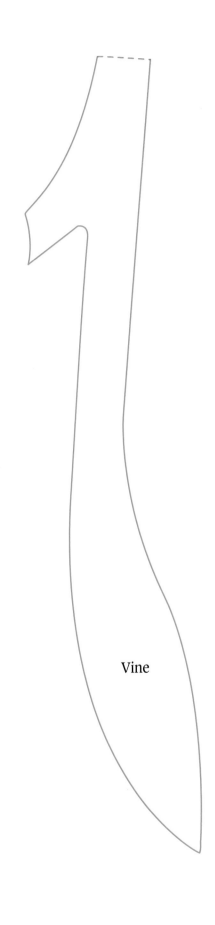

Vine

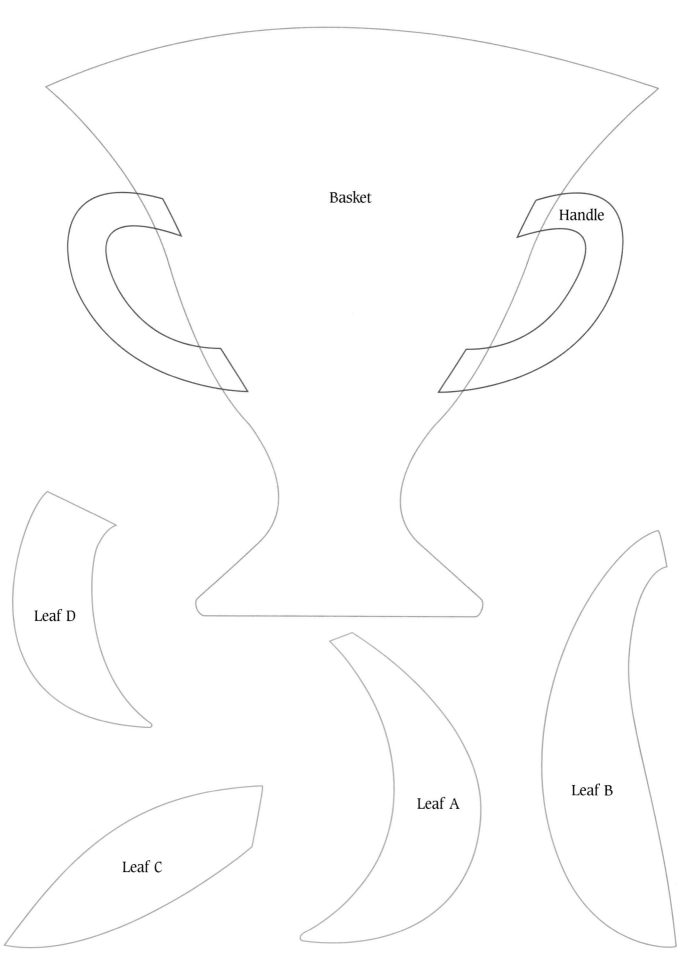

Basket

Handle

Leaf D

Leaf A

Leaf B

Leaf C

LULLABY ROSES

ROSE GARDEN QUILT

BLOCK SIZE: 9" x 9"
QUILT SIZE: 74" x 92"

YARDAGE REQUIREMENTS
Yardage is based on 45"w fabric.

- ☐ 7½ yards of white solid
- ▨ 2¼ yards of blue solid
- ▨ 2 yards of green solid
- ▨ 1½ yards of pink solid
- ■ ¼ yard of dark pink solid
  5 yards for backing
  1 yard for binding
  90" x 108" batting

CUTTING OUT THE PIECES
All measurements include a ¼" seam allowance. Follow Rotary Cutting, page 110, to cut fabric.

1. From white solid: ☐
   - Cut 115 selvage-to-selvage **strips** 2"w.
   - From 1 strip, cut 3 **squares** 2" x 2".

2. From blue solid: ▨
   - Cut 30 selvage-to-selvage **strips** 2"w.
   - From 1 strip, cut 1 **square** 2" x 2".

3. From green solid: ▨
   - Cut 22 selvage-to-selvage **strips** 2"w.

4. From pink solid: ▨
   - Cut 22 selvage-to-selvage **strips** 2"w.

5. From dark pink solid: ■
   - Cut 2 selvage-to-selvage **strips** 2"w.

ASSEMBLING THE QUILT TOP
Follow Piecing and Pressing, page 112, to make quilt top.

1. Sew strips together to make **Strip Set A**. Make 2 Strip Set A's. Cut across Strip Set A's at 2" intervals to make 32 **Unit 1's**.

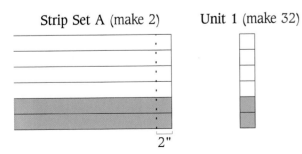

Strip Set A (make 2)   Unit 1 (make 32)

2"

2. Sew strips together to make **Strip Set B**. Make 2 Strip Set B's. Cut across Strip Set B's at 2" intervals to make 32 **Unit 2's**.

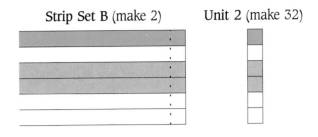

Strip Set B (make 2)   Unit 2 (make 32)

3. Sew strips together to make **Strip Set C**. Make 2 Strip Set C's. Cut across Strip Set C's at 2" intervals to make 32 **Unit 3's**.

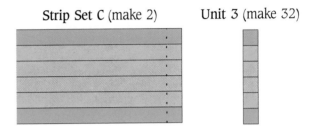

Strip Set C (make 2)   Unit 3 (make 32)

4. Sew strips together to make **Strip Set D**. Make 2 Strip Set D's. Cut across Strip Set D's at 2" intervals to make 32 **Unit 4's**.

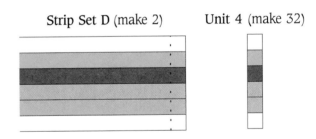

Strip Set D (make 2)   Unit 4 (make 32)

5. Sew strips together to make **Strip Set E**. Make 2 Strip Set E's. Cut across Strip Set E's at 2" intervals to make 32 **Unit 5's**.

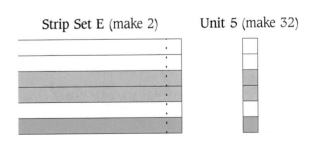

Strip Set E (make 2)   Unit 5 (make 32)

6. Sew **strips** together to make **Strip Set** F. Make 4 **Strip Set** F's. Cut across **Strip Set** F's at 2" intervals to make 64 **Unit** 6's.

Strip Set F (make 4)   Unit 6 (make 64)

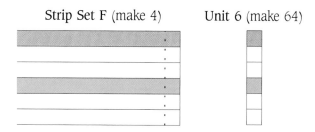

7. Sew **strips** together to make **Strip Set** G. Make 2 **Strip Set** G's. Cut across **Strip Set** G's at 2" intervals to make 28 **Unit** 7's.

Strip Set G (make 2)   Unit 7 (make 28)

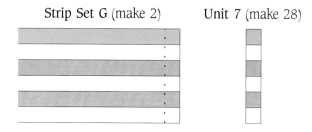

8. Sew **strips** together to make **Strip Set** H. Make 2 **Strip Set** H's. Cut across **Strip Set** H's at 2" intervals to make 28 **Unit** 8's.

Strip Set H (make 2)   Unit 8 (make 28)

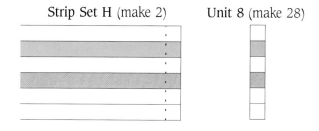

9. Sew **strips** together to make **Strip Set** I. Make 3 **Strip Set** I's. Cut across **Strip Set** I's at 2" intervals to make 44 **Unit** 9's.

Strip Set I (make 3)   Unit 9 (make 44)

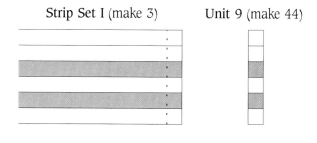

10. Sew **strips** together to make **Strip Set** J. Make 4 **Strip Set** J's. Cut across **Strip Set** J's at 2" intervals to make 76 **Unit** 10's.

Strip Set J (make 4)   Unit 10 (make 76)

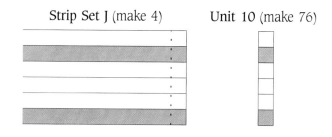

11. Sew **strips** together to make 1 **Strip Set** K. Cut across **Strip Set** at 2" intervals to make 21 **Unit** 11's.

Strip Set K (make 1)   Unit 11 (make 21)

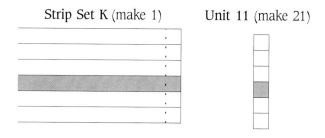

12. Sew **strips** together to make 1 **Strip Set** L. Cut across **Strip Set** L at 2" intervals to make 11 **Unit** 12's.

Strip Set L (make 1)   Unit 12 (make 11)

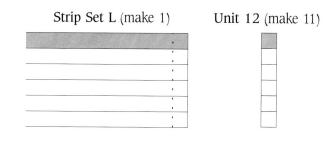

13. Sew **strips** together to make **Strip Set** M. Make 2 **Strip Set** M's. Cut across **Strip Set** M's at 2" intervals to make 42 **Unit** 13's.

Strip Set M (make 2)   Unit 13 (make 42)

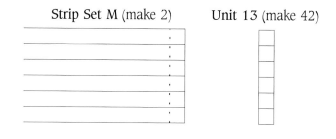

14. Sew **strips** together to make 1 **Strip Set N**. Cut across **Strip Set N** at 2" intervals to make 4 **Unit 14's**.

Strip Set N (make 1)   Unit 14 (make 4)

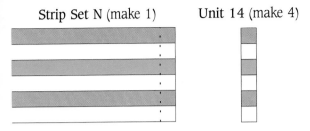

15. Sew **strips** together to make 1 **Strip Set O**. Cut across **Strip Set O** at 2" intervals to make 4 **Unit 15's**.

Strip Set O (make 1)   Unit 15 (make 4)

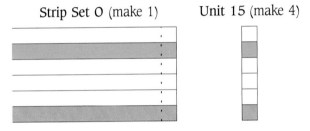

16. Sew **strips** together to make 1 **Strip Set P**. Cut across **Strip Set P** at 2" intervals to make 15 **Unit 16's**.

Strip Set P (make 1)   Unit 16 (make 15)

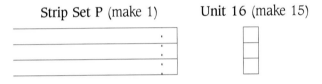

17. Sew **squares** together to make 1 **Unit 17**.

Unit 17 (make 1)

18. Referring to **Block** diagrams, sew **Units** together to make **Blocks**. Make number of each **Block** indicated above diagram.

Block A (make 32)   Block B (make 24)

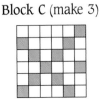

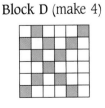

Block C (make 3)   Block D (make 4)

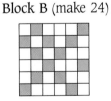

Block E (make 4)   Block F (make 3)

Block G (make 4)   Block H (make 7)

Block J (make 5)   Block K (make 5)

Block L (make 4)   Block M (make 1)

Block N (make 1)   Block O (make 2)

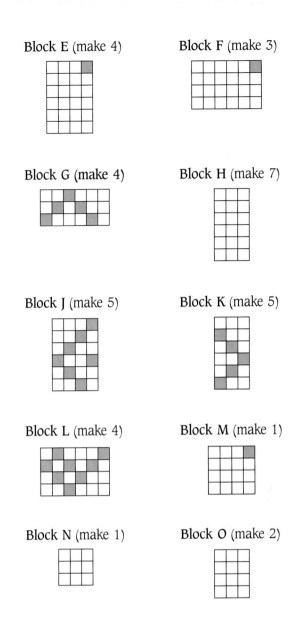

19. Arrange **Blocks** as shown in **Assembly Diagram**, page 106. Sew **Blocks** together to form horizontal rows; sew rows together to complete quilt top.

COMPLETING THE QUILT

1. Follow **Quilting**, page 117, to mark, layer, and quilt. Our quilt is hand quilted in a diagonal grid pattern.
2. Cut a 29" square of binding fabric. Follow **Binding**, page 121, to bind quilt using 2½"w bias binding with mitered corners.

Assembly Diagram

O	G	H	G	H	G	H	G	N
J	A	C	A	C	A	C	A	K
E	B	A	B	A	B	A	D	H
J	A	B	A	B	A	B	A	K
E	B	A	B	A	B	A	D	H
J	A	B	A	B	A	B	A	K
E	B	A	B	A	B	A	D	H
J	A	B	A	B	A	B	A	K
E	B	A	B	A	B	A	D	H
J	A	B	A	B	A	B	A	K
M	L	F	L	F	L	F	L	O

Quilt Top Diagram

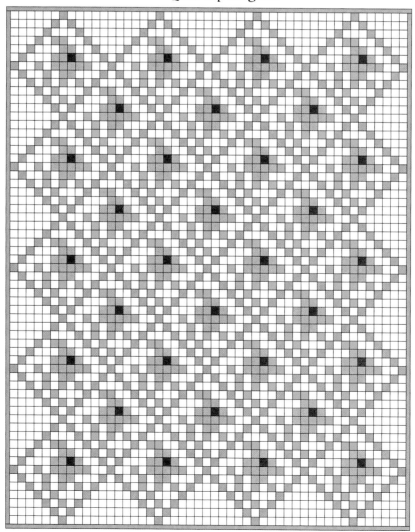

ROSEBUD BABY QUILT

BLOCK SIZE: 6" x 6"
QUILT SIZE: 26" x 38"

YARDAGE REQUIREMENTS
Yardage is based on 45"w fabric.

☐ 2 yards of white solid
◪ ⅝ yard of blue print
◪ ⅜ yard of green print
◪ ⅜ yard of pink print
◪ ⅛ yard of dark pink print
1 yard for backing
⅜ yard for binding
45" x 60" batting

CUTTING OUT THE PIECES
All measurements include a ¼" seam allowance. Follow Rotary Cutting, page 110, to cut fabric.

1. From white solid: ☐
   • Cut 39 selvage-to-selvage **strips** 1½"w.
   • From 1 strip, cut 3 **squares** 1½" x 1½".

2. From blue solid: ◪
   • Cut 9 selvage-to-selvage **strips** 1½"w.
   • From 1 strip, cut 1 **square** 1½" x 1½".

3. From green solid: ◪
   • Cut 6 selvage-to-selvage **strips** 1½"w.

4. From pink solid: ◪
   • Cut 6 selvage-to-selvage **strips** 1½"w.

5. From dark pink solid: ◪
   • Cut 1 selvage-to-selvage **strip** 1½"w.

ASSEMBLING THE QUILT TOP
Follow Piecing and Pressing, page 112, to make quilt top.

1. Cut each selvage-to-selvage **strip** in half at fabric fold so that all **strips** are approximately 21" long.
2. Referring to Steps 1 through 17 of **Rose Garden Quilt**, pages 103-105, sew **strips** together to make 1 each of **Strip Sets** A, B, C, D, E, G, H, K, L, N, and O, and 2 each of **Strip Sets** F, I, J, M, and P.
3. Cut across **Strip Sets** at 1½" intervals to make the following **Units**:

8 Unit 1's	18 Unit 9's
8 Unit 2's	22 Unit 10's
8 Unit 3's	11 Unit 11's
8 Unit 4's	5 Unit 12's
8 Unit 5's	18 Unit 13's
16 Unit 6's	2 Unit 14's
6 Unit 7's	2 Unit 15's
6 Unit 8's	15 Unit 16's

4. Referring to Step 18, page 105, of **Rose Garden Quilt** for **Block** diagrams, sew **Units** together to make the following **Blocks**.

8 Block A's	3 Block H's
4 Block B's	3 Block J's
1 Block C	3 Block K's
2 Block D's	2 Block L's
2 Block E's	1 Block M
1 Block F	1 Block N
2 Block G's	2 Block O's

5. Arrange **Blocks** as shown in **Assembly Diagram**. Sew **Blocks** together to form horizontal rows; sew rows together to complete **Quilt Top**.

COMPLETING THE QUILT
1. Follow **Quilting**, page 117, to mark, layer, and quilt. Our quilt is hand quilted in a diagonal grid pattern.
2. Follow **Binding**, page 121, to bind quilt using 2½"w straight-grain binding with overlapped corners.

Assembly Diagram

O	G	H	G	N
J	A	C	A	K
E	B	A	D	H
J	A	B	A	K
E	B	A	D	H
J	A	B	A	K
M	L	F	L	O

Quilt Top Diagram

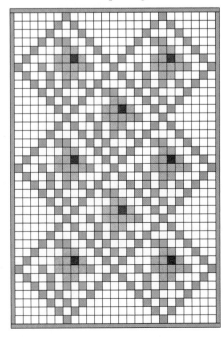

GENERAL INSTRUCTIONS

Complete instructions are given for making each of the quilts and other projects shown in this book. To make your quilting easier and more enjoyable, we encourage you to carefully read all of the general instructions, study the color photographs, and familiarize yourself with the individual project instructions before beginning a project.

QUILTING SUPPLIES

This list includes all the tools you need for basic quiltmaking, plus additional supplies used for special techniques. Unless otherwise specified, all items may be found in your favorite fabric store or quilt shop.

Batting — Batting is most commonly available in polyester, cotton, or a polyester/cotton blend (see **Choosing and Preparing the Batting**, page 119).

Cutting mat — A cutting mat is a special mat designed to be used with a rotary cutter. A mat that measures approximately 18" x 24" is a good size for most cutting.

Eraser — A soft white fabric eraser or white art eraser may be used to remove pencil marks from fabric. Do not use a colored eraser, as the dye may discolor fabric.

Iron — An iron with both steam and dry settings and a smooth, clean soleplate is necessary for proper pressing.

Marking tools — There are many different marking tools available (see **Marking Quilting Lines**, page 118). A silver quilter's pencil is a good marker for both light and dark fabrics.

Masking tape — Two widths of masking tape, 1"w and ¼"w, are helpful when quilting. The 1"w tape is used to secure the backing fabric to a flat surface when layering the quilt. The ¼"w tape may be used as a guide when outline quilting.

Needles — Two types of needles are used for hand sewing: *Betweens*, used for quilting, are short and strong for stitching through layered fabric and batting. *Sharps* are longer, thinner needles used for basting and other hand sewing. For *sewing machine needles*, we recommend size 10 to 14 or 70 to 90 universal (sharp-pointed) needles.

Paper-backed fusible web — This iron-on adhesive with paper backing is used to secure fabric cutouts to another fabric when appliquéing. If the cutouts will be stitched in place, purchase a lighter weight web that will not gum up your sewing machine needle. A heavier weight web is used for appliqués that are fused in place with no stitching.

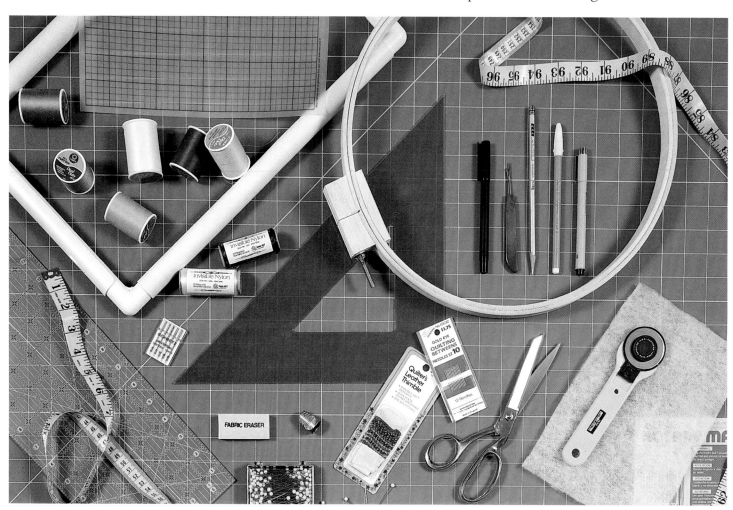

Permanent fine-point pen — A permanent pen is used to mark templates and stencils and to sign and date quilts. Test pen on fabric to make sure it will not bleed or wash out.

Pins — Straight pins made especially for quilting are extra long with large round heads. Glass head pins will stand up to occasional contact with a hot iron. Some quilters prefer extra-fine dressmaker's silk pins. If you are machine quilting, you will need a large supply of 1" long (size 01) rustproof safety pins for pin-basting.

Quilting hoop or frame — Quilting hoops and frames are designed to hold the 3 layers of a quilt together securely while you quilt. Many different types and sizes are available, including round and oval wooden hoops, frames made of rigid plastic pipe, and large floor frames made of either material. A 14" or 16" hoop allows you to quilt in your lap and makes your quilting portable.

Rotary cutter — The rotary cutter is the essential tool for quick-method quilting techniques. The cutter consists of a round, sharp blade mounted on a handle with a retractable blade guard for safety. It should be used only with a cutting mat and rotary cutting ruler. Two sizes are generally available; we recommend the larger (45 mm) size.

Rotary cutting ruler — A rotary cutting ruler is a thick, clear acrylic ruler made specifically for use with a rotary cutter. It should have accurate ⅛" crosswise and lengthwise markings and markings for 45° and 60° angles. A 6" x 24" ruler is a good size for most cutting. An additional 6" x 12" ruler or 12½" square ruler is helpful when cutting wider pieces. Many specialty rulers are available that make specific cutting tasks faster and easier.

Scissors — Although most fabric cutting will be done with a rotary cutter, sharp, high-quality scissors are still needed for some cutting. A separate pair of scissors for cutting paper and plastic is recommended. Smaller scissors are handy for clipping threads.

Seam ripper — A good seam ripper with a fine point is useful for removing stitching.

Sewing machine — A sewing machine that produces a good, even straight stitch is all that is necessary for most quilting. Zigzag stitch capability is necessary for Invisible Appliqué, page 115. Clean and oil your machine often and keep the tension set properly.

Stabilizer — Commercially made, non-woven material or paper stabilizer is placed behind background fabric when doing Invisible Appliqué, page 115, to provide a more stable stitching surface.

Tape measure — A flexible 120" long tape measure is helpful for measuring a quilt top before adding borders.

Template material — Sheets of translucent plastic, often pre-marked with a grid, are made especially for making templates and quilting stencils.

Thimble — A thimble is necessary when hand quilting. Thimbles are available in metal, plastic, or leather and in many sizes and styles. Choose a thimble that fits well and is comfortable.

Thread — Several types of thread are used for quiltmaking: General-purpose sewing thread is used for basting, piecing, and some appliquéing. Choose high-quality cotton or cotton-covered polyester thread in light and dark neutrals, such as ecru and grey, for your basic supplies. Quilting thread is stronger than general-purpose sewing thread, and some brands have a coating to make them slide more easily through the quilt layers. Some machine appliqué projects in this book use transparent monofilament (clear nylon) thread. Use a very fine (.004 mm) soft nylon thread that is not stiff or wiry. Choose clear nylon thread for white or light fabrics or smoke nylon thread for darker fabrics.

Triangle — A large plastic right-angle triangle (available in art and office supply stores) is useful in rotary cutting for making first cuts to "square up" raw edges of fabric and for checking to see that cuts remain at right angles to the fold.

Walking foot — A walking foot, or even-feed foot, is needed for straight-line machine quilting. This special foot will help all 3 layers move at the same rate over the feed dogs to provide a smoother quilted project.

FABRICS

SELECTING FABRICS

Choose high-quality, medium-weight 100% cotton fabrics such as broadcloth or calico. All-cotton fabrics hold a crease better, fray less, and are easier to quilt than cotton/polyester blends. All the fabrics for a quilt should be of comparable weight and weave. Check the end of the fabric bolt for fiber content and width.

The yardage requirements listed for each project are based on 45" wide fabric with a "usable" width of 42" after shrinkage and trimming selvages. Your actual usable width will probably vary slightly from fabric to fabric. Though most fabrics will yield 42" or more, if you find a fabric that you suspect will yield a narrower usable width, you will need to purchase additional yardage to compensate. Our recommended yardage lengths should be adequate for occasional resquaring of fabric when many cuts are required, but it never hurts to buy a little more fabric for insurance against a narrower usable width, the occasional cutting error, or to have on hand for making coordinating projects.

PREPARING FABRICS

All fabrics should be washed, dried, and pressed before cutting.

1. To check colorfastness before washing, cut a small piece of the fabric and place in a glass of hot water with a little detergent. Leave fabric in the water for a few minutes. Remove fabric from water and blot with white paper towels. If any color bleeds onto the towels, wash the fabric separately with warm water and detergent, then rinse until the water runs clear. If fabric continues to bleed, choose another fabric.
2. Unfold yardage and separate fabrics by color. To help reduce raveling, use scissors to snip a small triangle from each corner of your fabric pieces. Machine wash fabrics in warm water with a small amount of mild laundry detergent. Do not use fabric softener. Rinse well and then dry fabrics in the dryer, checking long fabric lengths occasionally to make sure they are not tangling.
3. To make ironing easier, remove fabrics from dryer while they are slightly damp. Refold each fabric lengthwise (as it was on the bolt) with wrong sides together and matching selvages. If necessary, adjust slightly at selvages so that fold lays flat. Press each fabric using a steam iron set on "Cotton."

ROTARY CUTTING

*Based on the idea that you can easily cut strips of fabric and then cut those strips into smaller pieces, rotary cutting has brought speed and accuracy to quiltmaking. Observe safety precautions when using the rotary cutter, since it is extremely sharp. Develop a habit of retracting the blade guard **just before** making a cut and closing it **immediately afterward,** before laying down the cutter.*

1. Follow **Preparing Fabrics**, this page, to wash, dry, and press fabrics.
2. Cut all strips from the selvage-to-selvage width of the fabric unless otherwise indicated in project instructions. Place fabric on the cutting mat, as shown in **Fig. 1**, with the fold of the fabric toward you. To straighten the uneven fabric edge, make the first "squaring up" cut by placing the right edge of the rotary cutting ruler over the left raw edge of the fabric. Place right-angle triangle (or another rotary cutting ruler) with the lower edge carefully aligned with the fold and the left edge against the ruler (**Fig. 1**). Hold the ruler firmly with your left hand, placing your little finger off the left edge to anchor the ruler. Remove the triangle, pick up the rotary cutter, and retract the blade guard. Using a smooth downward motion, make the cut by running the blade of the rotary cutter firmly along the right edge of the ruler (**Fig. 2**). **Always** cut in a direction **away** from your body and **immediately** close the blade guard after each cut.

Fig. 1

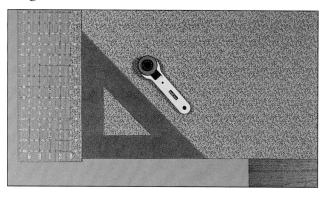

Fig. 2

3. To cut each of the strips required for a project, place the ruler over the cut edge of the fabric, aligning desired marking on the ruler with the cut edge (**Fig. 3**); make the cut. When cutting several strips from a single piece of fabric, it is important to occasionally use the ruler and triangle to ensure that cuts are still at a perfect right angle to the fold. If not, repeat Step 2 to straighten.

Fig. 3

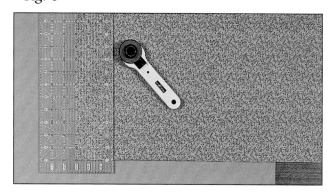

4. To square up selvage ends of a strip before cutting pieces, refer to **Fig. 4** and place folded strip on mat with selvage ends to your right. Aligning a horizontal marking on ruler with 1 long edge of strip, use rotary cutter to trim selvage to make end of strip square and even (**Fig. 4**). Turn strip (or entire mat) so that cut end is to your left before making subsequent cuts.

Fig. 4

5. Pieces such as rectangles and squares can now be cut from strips. (Cutting other shapes such as diamonds is discussed in individual project instructions.) Usually strips remain folded and pieces are cut in pairs after ends of strips are squared up. To cut squares or rectangles from a strip, place ruler over left end of strip, aligning desired marking on ruler with cut end of strip. To ensure perfectly square cuts, align a horizontal marking on ruler with 1 long edge of strip (Fig. 5) before making the cut.

Fig. 5

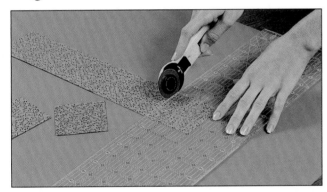

6. To cut 2 triangles from a square, cut square the size indicated in the project instructions. Cut square once diagonally to make 2 triangles (Fig. 6).

Fig. 6

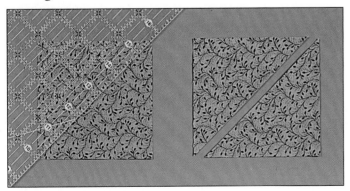

7. To cut 4 triangles from a square, cut square the size indicated in the project instructions. Cut square twice

diagonally to make 4 triangles (Fig. 7). You may find it helpful to use a small rotary cutting mat so that the mat can be turned to make second cut without disturbing fabric pieces.

Fig. 7

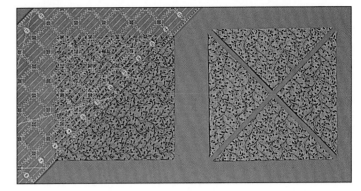

8. After some practice, you may want to try stacking up to 6 fabric layers when making cuts. When stacking strips, match long cut edges and follow Step 4, page 110, to square up ends of strip stack. Carefully turn stack (or entire mat) so that squared-up ends are to your left before making subsequent cuts. After cutting, check accuracy of pieces. Some shapes, such as diamonds, are more difficult to cut accurately in stacks.

9. In some cases, strips will be sewn together into strip sets before being cut into smaller units. When cutting a strip set, align a seam in strip set with a horizontal marking on the ruler to maintain square cuts (Fig. 8). We do not recommend stacking strip sets for rotary cutting.

Fig. 8

10. Most borders for quilts in this book are cut along the more stable lengthwise grain to minimize wavy edges caused by stretching. To remove selvages before cutting lengthwise strips, place fabric on mat with selvages to your left and squared-up end at bottom of mat. Placing ruler over selvage and using squared-up edge instead of fold, follow Step 2, page 110, to cut away selvages as you did raw edges (Fig. 9). After making a cut the length of the mat, move the next section of fabric to be cut onto the mat. Repeat until you have removed selvages from required length of fabric.

Fig. 9

11. After removing selvages, place ruler over left edge of fabric, aligning desired marking on ruler with cut edge of fabric. Make cuts as in Step 3. After each cut, move next section of fabric onto mat as in Step 10.

TEMPLATE CUTTING

Our full-sized piecing template patterns have 2 lines – a solid cutting line and a dashed line showing the ¼" seam allowance. Patterns for appliqué templates do not include seam allowances.

1. To make a template from a pattern, use a permanent fine-point pen to carefully trace pattern onto template plastic, making sure to transfer all alignment and grain line markings. Cut out template along inner edge of drawn line. Check template against original pattern for accuracy.
2. To make a template from a half pattern, use a ruler to draw a line down the center of a sheet of template plastic. Match grey dashed line of pattern to drawn line on plastic. Trace pattern onto plastic. Turn pattern over and trace again to complete. Cut out template as in Step 1.
3. To make a template from a one-quarter pattern, use a ruler to draw a line down the center of a sheet of template plastic. Turn plastic 90° and draw a line down the center, perpendicular to the first line. Match solid grey lines of pattern to intersection of lines on plastic. Trace pattern. Turn plastic and trace pattern in remaining corners. Cut out template as in Step 1.
4. To use a template, place template on wrong side of fabric (unless otherwise indicated in project instructions), aligning grain line on template with straight grain of fabric. Use a sharp fabric-marking pencil to draw around template. Transfer all alignment markings to fabric. Cut out fabric piece using scissors or rotary cutting equipment.

PIECING AND PRESSING

Precise cutting, followed by accurate piecing and careful pressing, will ensure that all the pieces of your quilt top fit together well.

PIECING

Set sewing machine stitch length for approximately 11 stitches per inch. Use a new, sharp needle suited for medium-weight woven fabric.

Use a neutral-colored general-purpose sewing thread (not quilting thread) in the needle and in the bobbin. Stitch first on a scrap of fabric to check upper and bobbin thread tension; make any adjustments necessary.

For good results, it is **essential** that you stitch with an **accurate** ¼" seam allowance. On many sewing machines, the measurement from the needle to the outer edge of the presser foot is ¼". If this is the case with your machine, the presser foot is your best guide. If not, measure ¼" from the needle and mark throat plate with a piece of masking tape. Special presser feet that are exactly ¼" wide are also available for most sewing machines.

When piecing, **always** place pieces **right sides together** and **match raw edges**; pin if necessary. (If using straight pins, remove the pins just before they reach the sewing machine needle.)

Chain Piecing

Chain piecing whenever possible will make your work go faster and will usually result in more accurate piecing. Stack the pieces you will be sewing beside your machine in the order you will need them and in a position that will allow you to easily pick them up. Pick up each pair of pieces, carefully place them together as they will be sewn, and feed them into the machine one after the other. Stop between each pair only long enough to pick up the next pair; don't cut thread between pairs (**Fig. 10**). After all pieces are sewn, cut threads, press, and go on to the next step, chain piecing when possible.

Fig. 10

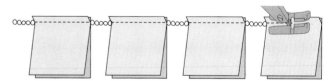

Sewing Strip Sets

When there are several strips to assemble into a strip set, first sew the strips together into pairs, then sew the pairs together to form the strip set. To help avoid distortion, sew 1 seam in 1 direction and then sew the next seam in the opposite direction (**Fig. 11**).

Fig. 11

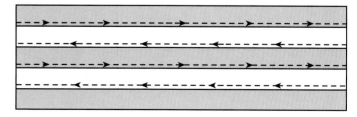

Sewing Across Seam Intersections

When sewing across the intersection of 2 seams, place pieces right sides together and match seams exactly, making sure seam allowances are pressed in opposite directions (**Fig. 12**). To prevent fabric from shifting, you may wish to pin in place.

Fig. 12

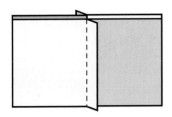

Sewing Bias Seams

Care should be used in handling and stitching bias edges since they stretch easily. After sewing the seam, carefully press seam allowance to 1 side, making sure not to stretch fabric.

Sewing Sharp Points

To ensure sharp points when joining triangular or diagonal pieces, stitch across the center of the "X" (shown in pink) formed on the wrong side by previous seams (**Fig. 13**).

Fig. 13

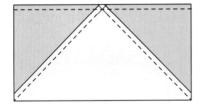

Making Triangle-Squares

The grid method for making triangle-squares is faster and more accurate than cutting and sewing individual triangles. Stitching before cutting the triangle-squares apart also prevents stretching the bias edges.

1. Follow project instructions to cut rectangles or squares of fabric for making triangle-squares. Place the indicated pieces right sides together and press.
2. On the wrong side of the lighter fabric, draw a grid of squares similar to that shown in **Fig. 14**. The size and number of squares are given in the project instructions.

Fig. 14

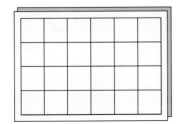

3. Following the example given in the project instructions, draw 1 diagonal line through each square in the grid (**Fig. 15**).

Fig. 15

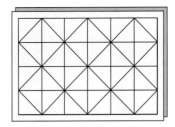

4. Stitch ¼" on each side of all diagonal lines. For accuracy, it may be helpful to first draw your stitching lines onto the fabric, especially if your presser foot is not your ¼" guide. In some cases, stitching may be done in a single continuous line. Project instructions include a diagram similar to **Fig. 16**, which shows stitching lines and the direction of the stitching.

Fig. 16

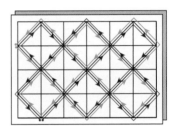

5. Use rotary cutter and ruler to cut along all drawn lines of the grid. Each square of the grid will yield 2 triangle-squares (**Fig. 17**).

Fig. 17

6. Carefully press triangle-squares open, pressing seam allowances toward darker fabric. Trim points of seam allowances that extend beyond edges of triangle-square (see **Fig. 22**).

113

Working with Diamonds and Set-in Seams

Piecing diamonds and sewing set-in seams require special handling. For best results, carefully follow the steps below.

1. When sewing 2 diamonds together, place pieces right sides together, carefully matching edges; pin. Mark a small dot ¼" from corner of 1 piece as shown in **Fig. 18**. Stitch pieces together in the direction shown, stopping at center of dot and backstitching.

Fig. 18

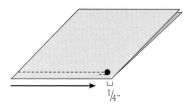

2. For best results, add side triangles, then corner squares to diamond sections. Mark corner of each piece to be set in with a small dot (**Fig. 19**).

Fig. 19

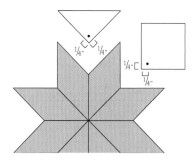

3. To sew first seam, match right sides and pin the triangle or square to the diamond on the left. Stitch seam from outer edge to the dot, backstitching at dot; clip threads (**Fig. 20**).

Fig. 20

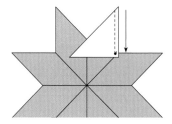

4. To sew the second seam, pivot the added triangle or square to match raw edges of next diamond. Beginning at dot, take 2 or 3 stitches, then backstitch, making sure not to backstitch into previous seam allowance. Continue stitching to outer edge (**Fig. 21**).

Fig. 21

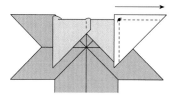

Trimming Seam Allowances

When sewing with diamond or triangle pieces, some seam allowances may extend beyond the edges of the sewn pieces. Trim away "dog ears" that extend beyond the edges of the sewn pieces (**Fig. 22**).

Fig. 22

PRESSING

Use a steam iron set on "Cotton" for all pressing. Press as you sew, taking care to prevent small folds along seamlines. Seam allowances are almost always pressed to one side, usually toward the darker fabric. However, to reduce bulk it may occasionally be necessary to press seam allowances toward the lighter fabric or even to press them open. In order to prevent a dark fabric seam allowance from showing through a light fabric, trim the darker seam allowance slightly narrower than the lighter seam allowance. To press long seams, such as those in long strip sets, without curving or other distortion, lay strips across the width of the ironing board.

APPLIQUÉ

PREPARING FUSIBLE APPLIQUÉS

Patterns are printed in reverse to enable you to use our speedy method of preparing appliqués. White or light-colored fabrics may need to be lined with fusible interfacing before applying fusible web to prevent darker fabrics from showing through.

1. Place paper-backed fusible web, web side down, over appliqué pattern. Use a pencil to trace pattern onto paper side of web as many times as indicated in project instructions for a single fabric. Repeat for additional patterns and fabrics.
2. Follow manufacturer's instructions to fuse traced patterns to wrong side of fabrics. Do not remove paper backing. (***Note:*** Some pieces may be given as measurements, such as a 2" x 4" rectangle, instead of drawn patterns. Fuse web to wrong side of the fabrics indicated for these pieces.)
3. Use scissors to cut out appliqué pieces along traced lines; use rotary cutting equipment to cut out appliqué pieces given as measurements. Remove paper backing from all pieces.

INVISIBLE APPLIQUÉ

This machine appliqué method uses clear nylon thread to secure the appliqué pieces. Transparent monofilament (clear nylon) thread is available in 2 colors: clear and smoke. Use clear on white or very light fabrics and smoke on darker colors.

1. Referring to diagram and/or photo, arrange prepared appliqués on the background fabric and follow manufacturer's instructions to fuse in place.
2. Pin a stabilizer, such as paper or any of the commercially available products, on wrong side of background fabric before stitching appliqués in place.
3. Thread sewing machine with transparent monofilament thread; use general-purpose thread that matches background fabric in bobbin.
4. Set sewing machine for a very narrow width (approximately 1/16") zigzag stitch and a short stitch length. You may find that loosening the top tension slightly will yield a smoother stitch.
5. Begin by stitching 2 or 3 stitches in place (drop feed dogs or set stitch length at 0) to anchor thread. Most of the zigzag stitch should be done on the appliqué with the right edges of the stitch falling at the very outside edge of the appliqué. Stitch over all exposed raw edges of appliqué pieces.
6. *(Note: Dots on **Figs. 23 - 28** indicate where to leave needle in fabric when pivoting.)* For **outside corners**, stitch just past the corner, stopping with the needle in **background** fabric (**Fig. 23**). Raise presser foot. Pivot project, lower presser foot, and stitch adjacent side (**Fig. 24**).

Fig. 23   Fig. 24

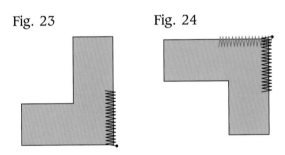

7. For **inside corners**, stitch just past the corner, stopping with the needle in **appliqué** fabric (**Fig. 25**). Raise presser foot. Pivot project, lower presser foot, and stitch adjacent side (**Fig. 26**).

Fig. 25   Fig. 26

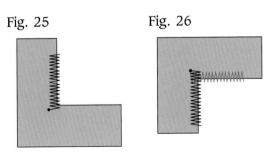

8. When stitching **outside** curves, stop with needle in **background** fabric. Raise presser foot and pivot project as needed. Lower presser foot and continue stitching, pivoting as often as necessary to follow curve (**Fig. 27**).

Fig. 27

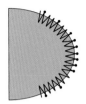

9. When stitching **inside** curves, stop with needle in **appliqué** fabric. Raise presser foot and pivot project as needed. Lower presser foot and continue stitching, pivoting as often as necessary to follow curve (**Fig. 28**).

Fig. 28

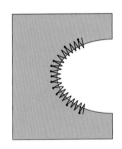

10. Do not backstitch at end of stitching. Pull threads to wrong side of background fabric; knot thread and trim ends.
11. Carefully tear away stabilizer.

MOCK HAND APPLIQUÉ

This technique uses the blindstitch on your sewing machine to achieve a look that closely resembles traditional hand appliqué. Using an updated method, appliqués are prepared with turned-under edges and then machine stitched to the background fabric. For best appliqué results, your sewing machine must have blindstitch capability with a variable stitch width. If your blindstitch width cannot be adjusted, you may still wish to try this technique to see if you are happy with the results. Some sewing machines have a narrower blindstitch width than others.

1. Follow project instructions to prepare appliqué pieces.
2. Thread needle of sewing machine with transparent monofilament thread; use general-purpose thread in bobbin in a color to match background fabric.
3. Set sewing machine for narrow blindstitch (just wide enough to catch 2 or 3 threads of the appliqué) and a very short stitch length (20 - 30 stitches per inch).

4. Arrange appliqué pieces on background fabric as described in project instructions. Use pins or hand baste to secure.
5. (*Note:* Follow Steps 6 - 9 of **Invisible Appliqué**, page 115, for needle position when pivoting.) Sew around edges of each appliqué so that the straight stitches fall on the background fabric very near the appliqué and the "hem" stitches barely catch the folded edge of the appliqué (**Fig. 29**).

Fig. 29

6. It is not necessary to backstitch at the beginning or end of stitching. End stitching by sewing ¼" over the first stitches. Trim thread ends close to the fabric.
7. To reduce bulk, turn project over and use scissors to cut away background fabric approximately ¼" inside stitching line of appliqué as shown in **Fig. 30**.

Fig. 30

wrong side

SATIN STITCH APPLIQUÉ

A good satin stitch is a smooth, almost solid line of zigzag stitching that covers the raw edges of appliqué pieces. Designs with layered appliqué pieces should be stitched beginning with the bottom pieces and ending with the pieces on top.

1. Follow Steps 1 and 2 of **Invisible Appliqué**, page 115.
2. Thread needle of sewing machine with general-purpose thread that coordinates or contrasts with appliqué fabric and use thread that matches background fabric in the bobbin. Set sewing machine for a medium width (approximately ⅛") zigzag stitch and a very short stitch length and refer to Steps 5 - 11 of **Invisible Appliqué** to stitch appliqués in place.

HAND APPLIQUÉ

*In this traditional hand appliqué method, the needle is used to turn the seam allowance under as you sew the appliqué to the background fabric using a **Blind Stitch**, page 124.*

1. Place template on right side of appliqué fabric. Use a pencil to lightly draw around template, leaving at least ½" between shapes; repeat for number of shapes specified in project instructions.
2. Cut out shapes approximately ³⁄₁₆" outside drawn line. Clip inside curves and points up to, but not through, drawn line. Arrange shapes on background fabric and pin or baste in place.
3. Thread a sharp needle with a single strand of general-purpose sewing thread; knot one end.
4. For each appliqué shape, begin on as straight an edge as possible and turn a small section of seam allowance to wrong side with needle, concealing drawn line. Use blind stitch to sew appliqué to background, turning under edge and stitching as you continue around shape. Do not turn under or stitch seam allowances that will be covered by other appliqué pieces.
5. Follow **Cutting Away Fabric Behind Appliqués**, this page, to reduce bulk.

CUTTING AWAY FABRIC BEHIND APPLIQUÉS

Hand quilting an appliquéd block will be easier if you are stitching through as few layers as possible. For this reason, or just to reduce bulk in your quilt, you may wish to cut away the background fabric behind appliqués. After stitching appliqués in place, turn block over and use sharp scissors or specially designed appliqué scissors to trim away background fabric approximately ³⁄₁₆" from stitching line. Take care not to cut appliqué fabric or stitches.

BORDERS

Borders cut along the lengthwise grain will lie flatter than borders cut along the crosswise grain. In most cases, our instructions for cutting borders for bed-size quilts include an extra 2" of length at each end for "insurance"; borders will be trimmed after measuring completed center section of quilt top.

ADDING SQUARED BORDERS
1. Mark the center of each edge of quilt top.
2. Squared borders are usually added to top and bottom, then side edges of the center section of a quilt top. To add top and bottom borders, measure across center of quilt top to determine length of borders (**Fig. 31**). Trim top and bottom borders to the determined length.

Fig. 31

3. Mark center of 1 long edge of top border. Matching center marks and raw edges, pin border to quilt top, easing in any fullness; stitch. Repeat for bottom border.
4. Measure center of quilt top, including attached borders, to determine length of side borders. Trim side borders to the determined length. Repeat Step 3 to add borders to quilt top (**Fig. 32**).

Fig. 32

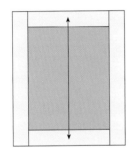

ADDING MITERED BORDERS
1. Mark the center of each edge of quilt top.
2. Mark center of 1 long edge of top border. Measure across center of quilt top (see **Fig. 31**). Matching center marks and raw edges, pin border to center of quilt top edge. Beginning at center of border, measure ½ the width of the quilt top in both directions and mark. Match marks on border with corners of quilt top and pin. Easing in any fullness, pin border to quilt top between center and corners.
Sew border to quilt top, beginning and ending seams **exactly** ¼" from each corner of quilt top and backstitching at beginning and end of stitching (**Fig. 33**).

Fig. 33

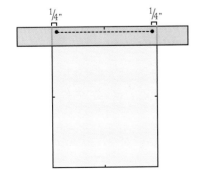

3. Repeat Step 2 to sew bottom, then side borders, to center section of quilt top. To temporarily move first 2 borders out of the way, fold and pin ends as shown in **Fig. 34**.

Fig. 34

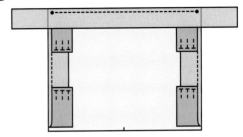

4. Fold 1 corner of quilt top diagonally with right sides together and matching edges. Use ruler to mark stitching line as shown in **Fig. 35**. Pin borders together along drawn line. Sew on drawn line, backstitching at beginning and end of stitching (**Fig. 36**).

Fig. 35

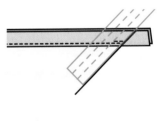

Fig. 36

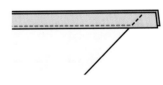

5. Turn mitered corner right side up. Check to make sure corner will lie flat with no gaps or puckers.
6. Trim seam allowance to ¼"; press to 1 side.
7. Repeat Steps 4 - 6 to miter each remaining corner.

QUILTING

*Quilting holds the 3 layers (top, batting, and backing) of the quilt together and can be done by hand or machine. Our project instructions tell you which method is used on each project and show you quilting diagrams that can be used as suggestions for marking quilting designs. Because marking, layering, and quilting are interrelated and may be done in different orders depending on circumstances, please read the entire **Quilting** section, pages 117 - 124, before beginning the quilting process on your project.*

TYPES OF QUILTING

In the Ditch

Quilting very close to a seamline (**Fig. 37**) or appliqué (**Fig. 38**) is called "in the ditch" quilting. This type of quilting does not need to be marked and is indicated on our quilting diagrams with blue lines close to seamlines. When quilting in the ditch, quilt on the side **opposite** the seam allowance.

Fig. 37   Fig. 38

 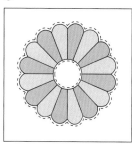

Outline Quilting

Quilting approximately ¼" from a seam or appliqué is called "outline" quilting (**Fig. 39**). This type of quilting is indicated on our quilting diagrams by blue lines a short distance from seamlines. Outline quilting may be marked, or you may place ¼"w masking tape along seamlines and quilt along the opposite edge of the tape. (Do not leave tape on quilt longer than necessary, since it may leave an adhesive residue.)

Fig. 39

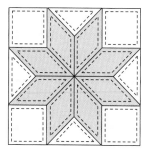

Ornamental Quilting

Quilting decorative lines or designs is called "ornamental" quilting (**Fig. 40**). Ornamental quilting is indicated on our quilting diagrams by blue lines. This type of quilting should be marked before you baste quilt layers together.

Fig. 40

MARKING QUILTING LINES

Fabric marking pencils, various types of chalk markers, and fabric marking pens with inks that disappear with exposure to air or water are readily available and work well for different applications. Lead pencils work well on light-color fabrics, but marks may be difficult to remove. White pencils work well on dark-color fabrics, and silver pencils show up well on many colors. Since chalk rubs off easily, it's a good choice if you are marking as you quilt. Fabric marking pens make more durable and visible markings, but the marks should be carefully removed according to manufacturer's instructions. Press down only as hard as necessary to make a visible line.

When you choose to mark your quilt, whether before or after the layers are basted together, is also a factor in deciding which marking tool to use. If you mark with chalk or a chalk pencil, handling the quilt during basting may rub off the markings. Intricate or ornamental designs may not be practical to mark as you quilt; mark these designs before basting using a more durable marker.

To choose marking tools, take all these factors into consideration and **test** different markers **on scrap fabric** until you find the one that gives the desired result.

USING QUILTING STENCILS

A wide variety of precut quilting stencils, as well as entire books of quilting patterns, are available. Using a stencil makes it easier to mark intricate or repetitive designs on your quilt top.

1. To make a stencil from a pattern, center template plastic over pattern and use a permanent marker to trace pattern onto plastic.
2. Use a craft knife with a single or double blade to cut narrow slits along traced lines (**Fig. 41**).

Fig. 41

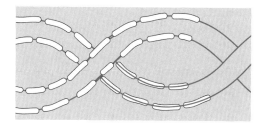

3. Use desired marking tool and stencil to mark quilting lines.

CHOOSING AND PREPARING THE BACKING

To allow for slight shifting of the quilt top during quilting, the backing should be approximately 4" larger on all sides for a bed-size quilt top or approximately 2" larger on all sides for a wall hanging. Yardage requirements listed for quilt backings are calculated for 45"w fabric. If you are making a bed-size quilt, using 90"w or 108"w fabric for the backing may eliminate piecing. To piece a backing using 45"w fabric, use the following instructions.

1. Measure length and width of quilt top; add 8" (4" for a wall hanging) to each measurement.
2. If quilt top is 76"w or less, cut backing fabric into 2 lengths slightly longer than the determined **length** measurement. Trim selvages. Place lengths with right sides facing and sew long edges together, forming a tube (**Fig. 42**). Match seams and press along 1 fold (**Fig. 43**). Cut along pressed fold to form a single piece (**Fig. 44**).

Fig. 42   Fig. 43   Fig. 44

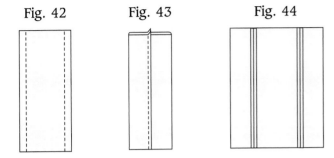

3. If quilt top is more than 76"w, cut backing fabric into 3 lengths slightly longer than the determined **width** measurement. Trim selvages. Sew long edges together to form a single piece.
4. Trim backing to correct size, if necessary, and press seam allowances open.

CHOOSING AND PREPARING THE BATTING

Choosing the right batting will make your quilting job easier. For fine hand quilting, choose a low-loft batting in any of the fiber types described here. Machine quilters will want to choose a low-loft batting that is all cotton or a cotton/polyester blend because the cotton helps "grip" the layers of the quilt. If the quilt is to be tied, a high-loft batting, sometimes called extra-loft or fat batting, is a good choice.

Batting is available in many different fibers. Bonded polyester batting is one of the most popular batting types. It is treated with a protective coating to stabilize the fibers and to reduce "bearding," a process in which batting fibers work their way out through the quilt fabrics. Other batting options include cotton/polyester batting, which combines the best of both polyester and cotton battings; all-cotton batting, which must be quilted more closely than polyester batting; and wool and silk battings, which are generally more expensive and usually only dry-cleanable.

Whichever batting you choose, read the manufacturer's instructions closely for any special notes on care or preparation. When you're ready to use your chosen batting in a project, cut batting the same size as the prepared backing.

LAYERING THE QUILT
1. Examine wrong side of quilt top closely; trim any seam allowances and clip any threads that may show through the front of the quilt. Press quilt top.
2. If quilt top is to be marked before layering, mark quilting lines (see **Marking Quilting Lines**, page 118).
3. Place backing **wrong** side up on a flat surface. Use masking tape to tape edges of backing to surface. Place batting on top of backing fabric. Smooth batting gently, being careful not to stretch or tear. Center quilt top **right** side up on batting.
4. If hand quilting, begin in the center and work toward the outer edges to hand baste all layers together. Use long stitches and place basting lines approximately 4" apart (**Fig. 45**). Smooth fullness or wrinkles toward outer edges.

Fig. 45

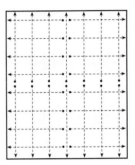

5. If machine quilting, use 1" rustproof safety pins to "pin-baste" all layers together, spacing pins approximately 4" apart. Begin at the center and work toward the outer edges to secure all layers. If possible, place pins away from areas that will be quilted, although pins may be removed as needed when quilting.

HAND QUILTING
The quilting stitch is a basic running stitch that forms a broken line on the quilt top and backing. Stitches on the quilt top and backing should be straight and equal in length.

1. Secure center of quilt in hoop or frame. Check quilt top and backing to make sure they are smooth. To help prevent puckers, always begin quilting in the center of the quilt and work toward the outside edges.
2. Thread needle with an 18" - 20" length of quilting thread; knot 1 end. Using a thimble, insert needle into quilt top and batting approximately ½" from where you wish to begin quilting. Bring needle up at the point where you wish to begin (**Fig. 46**); when knot catches on quilt top, give thread a quick, short pull to "pop" knot through fabric into batting (**Fig. 47**).

Fig. 46

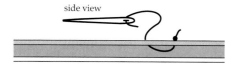

side view

Fig. 47

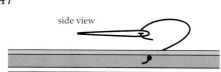

side view

3. Holding the needle with your sewing hand and placing your other hand underneath the quilt, use thimble to push the tip of the needle down through all layers. As soon as needle touches your finger underneath, use that finger to push the tip of the needle only back up through the layers to top of quilt. (The amount of the needle showing above the fabric determines the length of the quilting stitch.) Referring to **Fig. 48**, rock the needle up and down, taking 3 - 6 stitches before bringing the needle and thread completely through the layers. Check the back of the quilt to make sure stitches are going through all layers. When quilting through a seam allowance or quilting a curve or corner, you may need to make 1 stitch at a time.

Fig. 48

4. When you reach the end of your thread, knot thread close to the fabric and "pop" knot into batting; clip thread close to fabric.

5. Stop and move your hoop as often as necessary. You do not have to tie a knot every time you move your hoop; you may leave the thread dangling and pick it up again when you return to that part of the quilt.

MACHINE QUILTING

The following instructions are for straight-line quilting, which requires a walking foot or even-feed foot. The term "straight-line" is somewhat deceptive, since curves (especially gentle ones) as well as straight lines can be stitched with this technique.

1. Wind your sewing machine bobbin with general-purpose thread that matches the quilt backing. Do not use quilting thread. Thread the needle of your machine with transparent monofilament thread if you want your quilting to blend with your quilt top fabrics. Use decorative thread, such as a metallic or contrasting-color general-purpose thread, when you want the quilting lines to stand out more. Set the stitch length for 6 - 10 stitches per inch and attach the walking foot to sewing machine.

2. After pin-basting, decide which section of the quilt will have the longest continuous quilting line, oftentimes the area from center top to center bottom. Leaving the area exposed where you will place your first line of quilting, roll up each edge of the quilt to help reduce the bulk, keeping fabrics smooth. Smaller projects may not need to be rolled.

3. Start stitching at beginning of longest quilting line, using very short stitches for the first ¼" to "lock" beginning of quilting line. Stitch across project, using one hand on each side of the walking foot to slightly spread the fabric and to guide the fabric through the machine. Lock stitches at end of quilting line.

4. Continue machine quilting, stitching longer quilting lines first to stabilize the quilt before moving on to other areas.

MACHINE STIPPLE QUILTING

The term "stipple quilting" refers to extensive, closely spaced quilting, usually used to fill in background areas of pieced or appliquéd blocks.

1. Wind your sewing machine bobbin with general-purpose thread that matches the quilt backing. Do not use quilting thread. Thread the needle of your machine with transparent monofilament thread if you want your quilting to blend with your quilt top. Use decorative thread, such as metallic or contrasting-colored general-purpose thread, when you want the quilting lines to stand out.

2. For random stipple quilting, use a darning foot, drop or cover feed dogs, and set stitch length at zero. Stitch 2 or 3 stitches in place to lock thread. Place hands lightly on quilt on either side of darning foot.

3. Begin stitching in a meandering pattern (**Fig. 49**), guiding the quilt with your hands. The object is to make stitches of similar length and to not sew over previous stitching lines. The movement of your hands determines the stitch length; it takes practice to coordinate your hand motions and the pressure you put on the foot pedal, so go slowly at first.

Fig. 49

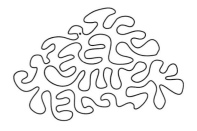

4. Continue machine quilting, filling in one open area of the quilt before moving on to another area and locking the thread again at end of each line of stitching by sewing 2 or 3 stitches in place.

BINDING

Binding encloses the raw edges of your quilt. Because of its stretchiness, bias binding works well for binding projects with curves or rounded corners and tends to lie smooth and flat in any given circumstance. It is also more durable than other types of binding. Binding may also be cut from the straight lengthwise or crosswise grain of the fabric. You will find that straight-grain binding works well for projects with straight edges.

MAKING CONTINUOUS BIAS STRIP BINDING

Bias strips for binding can simply be cut and pieced to the desired length. However, when a long length of binding is needed, the "continuous" method is quick and accurate.

1. Cut a square from binding fabric the size indicated in the project instructions. Cut square in half diagonally to make 2 triangles.
2. With right sides together and using a ¼" seam allowance, sew triangles together (**Fig. 50**); press seam allowance open.

Fig. 50

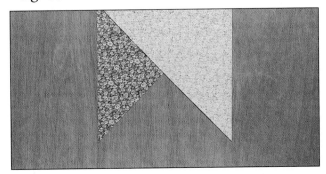

3. On wrong side of fabric, draw lines the width of the binding as specified in the project instructions, usually 2½" (**Fig. 51**). Cut off any remaining fabric less than this width.

Fig. 51

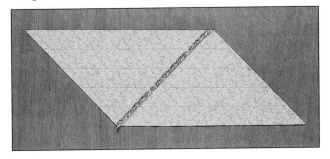

4. With right sides inside, bring short edges together to form a tube; match raw edges so that first drawn line of top section meets second drawn line of bottom section (**Fig. 52**).

Fig. 52

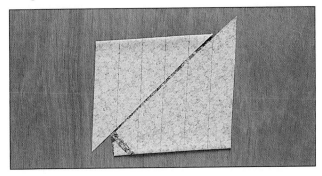

5. Carefully pin edges together by inserting pins through drawn lines at the point where drawn lines intersect, making sure the pins go through intersections on both sides. Using a ¼" seam allowance, sew edges together. Press seam allowance open.
6. To cut continuous strip, begin cutting along first drawn line (**Fig. 53**). Continue cutting along drawn line around tube.

Fig. 53

7. Trim ends of bias strip square.
8. Matching wrong sides and raw edges, press bias strip in half lengthwise to complete binding.

MAKING STRAIGHT-GRAIN BINDING

1. To determine length of strip needed if attaching binding with mitered corners, measure edges of the quilt and add 12".
2. To determine lengths of strips needed if attaching binding with overlapped corners, measure each edge of quilt; add 3" to each measurement.
3. Cut lengthwise or crosswise strips of binding fabric the determined length and the width called for in the project instructions. Strips may be pieced to achieve the necessary length.
4. Matching wrong sides and raw edges, press strip(s) in half lengthwise to complete binding.

ATTACHING BINDING WITH MITERED CORNERS

1. Press 1 end of binding diagonally (**Fig. 54**).

Fig. 54

2. Beginning with pressed end several inches from a corner, lay binding around quilt to make sure that seams in binding will not end up at a corner. Adjust placement if necessary. Matching raw edges of binding to raw edge of quilt top, pin binding to right side of quilt along 1 edge.
3. When you reach the first corner, mark ¼" from corner of quilt top (**Fig. 55**).

Fig. 55

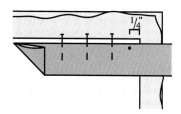

4. Using a ¼" seam allowance, sew binding to quilt, backstitching at beginning of stitching and when you reach the mark (**Fig. 56**). Lift needle out of fabric and clip thread.

Fig. 56

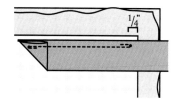

5. Fold binding as shown in **Figs. 57** and **58** and pin binding to adjacent side, matching raw edges. When you reach the next corner, mark ¼" from edge of quilt top.

Fig. 57   Fig. 58

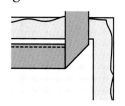 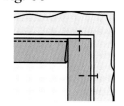

6. Backstitching at edge of quilt top, sew pinned binding to quilt (**Fig. 59**); backstitch when you reach the next mark. Lift needle out of fabric and clip thread.

Fig. 59

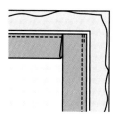

7. Repeat Steps 5 and 6 to continue sewing binding to quilt until binding overlaps beginning end by approximately 2". Trim excess binding.
8. If using 2½"w binding (finished size ½"), trim backing and batting a scant ¼" larger than quilt top so that batting and backing will fill the binding when it is folded over to the quilt backing. If using narrower binding, trim backing and batting even with edges of quilt top.
9. On 1 edge of quilt, fold binding over to quilt backing and pin pressed edge in place, covering stitching line (**Fig. 60**). On adjacent side, fold binding over, forming a mitered corner (**Fig. 61**). Repeat to pin remainder of binding in place.

Fig. 60   Fig. 61

10. Blindstitch binding to backing, taking care not to stitch through to front of quilt.

ATTACHING BINDING WITH OVERLAPPED CORNERS

1. Matching raw edges and using a ¼" seam allowance, sew a length of binding to top and bottom edges on right side of quilt.
2. If using 2½"w binding (finished size ½"), trim backing and batting **from top and bottom edges** a scant ¼" larger than quilt top so that batting and backing will fill the binding when it is folded over to the quilt backing. If using narrower binding, trim backing and batting even with edges of quilt top.
3. Trim ends of top and bottom binding even with edges of quilt top. Fold binding over to quilt backing and pin pressed edges in place, covering stitching line (**Fig. 62**); blindstitch binding to backing.

Fig. 62

4. Leaving approximately 1½" of binding at each end, stitch a length of binding to each side edge of quilt. Trim backing and batting as in Step 2.

5. Trim each end of binding ½" longer than bound edge. Fold each end of binding over to quilt backing (**Fig. 63**); pin in place. Fold binding over to quilt backing and blindstitch in place, taking care not to stitch through to front of quilt.

Fig. 63

MAKING A HANGING SLEEVE

Attaching a hanging sleeve to the back of your wall hanging or quilt before the binding is added allows you to display your completed project on a wall.

1. Measure the width of the wall hanging top and subtract 1". Cut a piece of fabric 7"w by the determined measurement.
2. Press short edges of fabric piece ¼" to wrong side; press edges ¼" to wrong side again and machine stitch in place.
3. Matching wrong sides, fold piece in half lengthwise to form a tube.
4. Follow project instructions to sew binding to quilt top and to trim backing and batting. Before blindstitching binding to backing, match raw edges and stitch hanging sleeve to center top edge on back of wall hanging.
5. Finish binding wall hanging, treating the hanging sleeve as part of the backing.
6. Blindstitch bottom of hanging sleeve to backing, taking care not to stitch through to front of quilt.
7. Insert dowel or slat into hanging sleeve.

SIGNING AND DATING YOUR QUILT

Your completed quilt is a work of art and should be signed and dated. There are many different ways to do this, and you should pick a method that reflects the style of the quilt, the occasion for which it was made, and your own particular talents.

The following suggestions may give you an idea for recording the history of your quilt for future generations.

- Embroider your name, the date, and any additional information on the quilt top or backing. You may choose embroidery floss colors that closely match the fabric you are working on, such as white floss on a white border, or contrasting colors may be used.

- Make a label from muslin and use a permanent marker to write your information. Your label may be as plain or as fancy as you wish. Stitch the label to the back of the quilt.
- Chart a cross-stitch label design that includes the information you wish and stitch it in colors that complement the quilt. Stitch the finished label to the quilt backing.

PILLOW FINISHING

Any quilt block may be made into a pillow. If desired, you may add welting and/or a ruffle to the pillow top before sewing the pillow top and back together.

ADDING WELTING TO PILLOW TOP

1. To make welting, use bias strip indicated in project instructions. (Or measure edges of pillow top and add 4". Measure circumference of cord and add 2". Cut a bias strip of fabric the determined measurement, piecing if necessary.)
2. Lay cord along center of bias strip on wrong side of fabric; fold strip over cord. Using a zipper foot, machine baste along length of strip close to cord. Trim seam allowance to the width you will use to sew pillow top and back together (see Step 2 of **Making the Pillow**, page 124).
3. Matching raw edges and beginning and ending 3" from ends of welting, baste welting to right side of pillow top. To make turning corners easier, clip seam allowance of welting at pillow top corners.
4. Remove approximately 3" of seam at 1 end of welting; fold fabric away from cord. Trim remaining end of welting so that cord ends meet exactly (**Fig. 64**).

Fig. 64

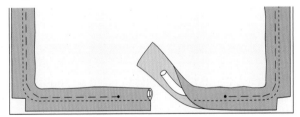

5. Fold short edge of welting fabric ½" to wrong side; fold fabric back over area where ends meet (**Fig. 65**).

Fig. 65

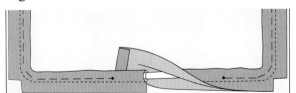

6. Baste remainder of welting to pillow top close to cord (Fig. 66).

Fig. 66

7. Follow **Making the Pillow** to complete pillow.

ADDING RUFFLE TO PILLOW TOP

1. To make ruffle, use fabric strip indicated in project instructions.
2. Matching right sides, use a ¼" seam allowance to sew short edges of ruffle together to form a large circle; press seam allowance open. To form ruffle, fold along length with wrong sides together and raw edges matching; press.
3. To gather ruffle, place quilting thread ¼" from raw edge of ruffle. Using a medium-width zigzag stitch with medium stitch length, stitch over quilting thread, being careful not to catch quilting thread in stitching. Pull quilting thread, drawing up gathers to fit pillow top.
4. Matching raw edges, baste ruffle to right side of pillow top.
5. Follow **Making the Pillow** to complete pillow.

MAKING THE PILLOW

1. For pillow back, cut a piece of fabric the same size as pieced and quilted pillow top.
2. Place pillow back and pillow top right sides together. The seam allowance width you use will depend on the construction of the pillow top. If the pillow top has borders on which the finished width of the border is not crucial, use a ½" seam allowance for durability. If the pillow top is pieced so that a wider seam allowance would interfere with the design, use a ¼" seam allowance. Using the determined seam allowance (or stitching as close as possible to welting), sew pillow top and back together, leaving an opening at bottom edge for turning.
3. Turn pillow right side out, carefully pushing corners outward. Stuff with polyester fiberfill or pillow form and sew final closure by hand.

EMBROIDERY STITCHES
TRADITIONAL EMBROIDERY STITCHES
Blindstitch
Come up at 1. Go down at 2 and come up at 3 (Fig. 67). Length of stitches may be varied as desired.

Fig. 67

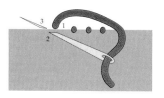

Blanket Stitch
Come up at 1. Go down at 2 and come up at 3, keeping thread below point of needle (**Fig. 68**). Continue working as shown in **Fig. 69**.

Fig. 68   Fig. 69

Feather Stitch
Come up at 1. Go down at 2 and come up at 3, keeping floss below point of needle (**Fig. 70**). Alternate stitches from right to left, keeping stitches symmetrical (**Fig. 71**).

Fig. 70   Fig. 71

French Knot
Come at 1. Wrap thread once around needle and insert needle at 2, holding end of thread with non-stitching fingers (**Fig. 72**). Tighten knot; then pull needle through, holding floss until it must be released. For larger knot, use more strands; wrap only once.

Fig. 72

Herringbone Stitch
Coming up at odd numbers and going down at even numbers, work evenly spaced stitches as shown in Fig. 73.

Fig. 73

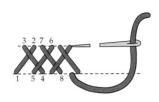

Lazy Daisy Stitch
Bring needle up at 1; take needle down again at 1 to form a loop and bring needle up at 2. Keeping loop below point of needle (Fig. 74), take needle down at 3 to anchor loop (Fig. 75).

Fig. 74　　　　　Fig. 75

Running Stitch
The running stitch consists of a series of straight stitches with the stitch length equal to the space between stitches (Fig. 76).

Fig. 76

Straight Stitch
Come up at 1 and go down at 2 (Fig. 77). Length of stitches may be varied as desired.

Fig. 77

Stem Stitch
Come up at 1. Keeping thread below the stitching line, go down at 2 and come up at 3. Go down at 4 and come up at 5 (Fig. 78).

Fig. 78

SILK RIBBON EMBROIDERY STITCHES
To retain the dimensional quality of silk ribbon, be careful not to pull it too tightly or twist it too much when stitching.

To thread needle, cut an approximate 14" length of ribbon. Thread 1 end of ribbon through eye of needle. Pierce same end of ribbon about ¼" from end with point of needle (Fig. 79). Pull on remaining ribbon end, locking ribbon into eye of needle (Fig. 80).

Fig. 79　　　　　Fig. 80

To begin and end a length of ribbon, form a soft knot in ribbon by folding ribbon end about ¼" and piercing needle through both layers (Fig. 81). Gently pull ribbon through to form a knot (Fig. 82). To end, secure ribbon on wrong side of fabric by tying a knot.

Fig. 81　　　　　Fig. 82

Couched Ribbon Bow
Cut a piece of ribbon desired length. Fold ribbon in half and mark fold. Sew ribbon to fabric at mark (Fig. 83). Tie ribbon into a bow. Arrange loops and streamers as desired and anchor with embroidery floss **French Knots** (Fig. 84).

Fig. 83　　　　　Fig. 84

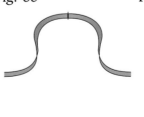

French Knot

Follow instructions for traditional embroidery **French Knot**, page 124, but wrap ribbon around needle twice (**Fig. 85**).

Fig. 85

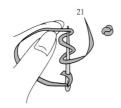

Japanese Ribbon Stitch

Bring needle up at 1. Lay ribbon flat on fabric and take needle down at 2, piercing ribbon (**Fig. 86**). Gently pull needle through to back. Ribbon will curl at end of stitch as shown in **Fig. 87**.

Fig. 86   Fig. 87

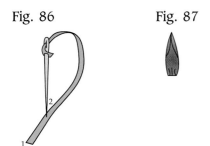

Lazy Daisy Stitch

Bring needle up at 1; take needle down again at 1 to form a loop and bring needle up at 2, allowing ribbon to twist and keeping ribbon below point of needle (**Fig. 88**). Take needle down at 3 to anchor loop.

Fig. 88

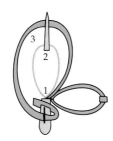

Loop Stitch

Bring needle up at 1. Use a large blunt needle or toothpick to hold ribbon flat on fabric. Take needle down at 2, using blunt needle to hold ribbon flat while pulling ribbon through to back of fabric (**Fig. 89**). Leave blunt needle in loop until needle is brought up at 3 for next loop (**Fig. 90**). Use embroidery floss to tack large loops in place.

Fig. 89   Fig. 90

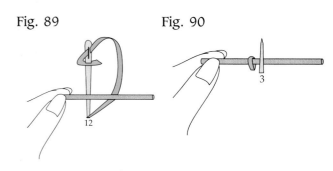

Spider Web Rose

Use a removable fabric marking pen to lightly draw a circle the desired size for rose. For anchor stitches, use 1 strand of embroidery floss to work 5 straight stitches from edge of circle to center, bringing needle up at odd numbers and taking needle down at even numbers (**Fig. 91**). For ribbon petals, bring needle up at center of anchor stitches; weave ribbon over and under anchor stitches (**Fig. 92**), keeping ribbon loose and allowing ribbon to twist. Continue to weave ribbon until anchor stitches are covered. Take needle down to wrong side of fabric.

Fig. 91   Fig. 92

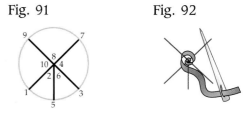

Wrapped Straight Stitch

Begin with a straight stitch. Bring needle up again at 1. Keeping ribbon flat, wrap ribbon around stitch without catching fabric or stitch (**Fig. 93**). To end stitch, take needle down at 2 (**Fig. 94**).

Fig. 93   Fig. 94

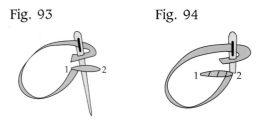

GLOSSARY

Appliqué — A cut-out fabric shape that is secured to a larger background. Also refers to the technique of securing the cut-out pieces.

Backing — The back or bottom layer of a quilt, sometimes called the "lining."

Backstitch — A reinforcing stitch taken at the beginning and end of a seam to secure stitches.

Basting — Large running stitches used to temporarily secure pieces or layers of fabric together. Basting is removed after permanent stitching.

Batting — The middle layer of a quilt that provides the insulation and warmth as well as the thickness.

Bias — The diagonal (45° for true bias) grain of fabric in relation to crosswise or lengthwise grain (see **Fig. 95**).

Binding — The fabric strip used to enclose the raw edges of the layered and quilted quilt. Also refers to the technique of finishing quilt edges in this way.

Blindstitch — A method of hand sewing an opening closed so that it is invisible.

Border — Strips of fabric that are used to frame a quilt top.

Chain piecing — A machine-piecing method consisting of joining pairs of pieces one after the other by feeding them through the sewing machine without cutting the thread between the pairs.

Grain — The direction of the threads in woven fabric. "Crosswise grain" refers to the threads running from selvage to selvage. "Lengthwise grain" refers to the threads running parallel to the selvages (**Fig. 95**).

Fig. 95

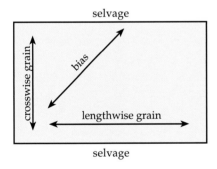

Machine baste — To baste using a sewing machine set at a long stitch length.

Miter — A method used to finish corners of quilt borders or bindings consisting of joining fabric pieces at a 45° angle.

Piecing — Sewing together the pieces of a quilt design to form a quilt block or an entire quilt top.

Pin basting — Using rustproof safety pins to secure the layers of a quilt together prior to machine quilting.

Quilt blocks — Pieced or appliquéd sections that are sewn together to form a quilt top.

Quilt top — The decorative part of a quilt that is layered on top of the batting and backing.

Quilting — The stitching that holds together the 3 quilt layers (top, batting, and backing); or, the entire process of making a quilt.

Sashing — Strips or blocks of fabric that separate individual blocks in a quilt top.

Seam allowance — The distance between the seam and the cut edge of the fabric. In quilting, the seam allowance is usually ¼".

Selvages — The 2 finished lengthwise edges of fabric (see **Fig. 95**). Selvages should be trimmed from fabric before cutting.

Set (or Setting) — The arrangement of the quilt blocks as they are sewn together to form the quilt top.

Setting squares — Squares of plain (unpieced) fabric set between pieced or appliquéd quilt blocks in a quilt top.

Setting triangles — Triangles of fabric used around the outside of a diagonally set quilt top to fill in between outer squares and border or binding.

Stencil — A pattern used for marking quilting lines.

Straight grain — The crosswise or lengthwise grain of fabric (see **Fig. 95**). The lengthwise grain has the least amount of stretch.

Strip set — Two or more strips of fabric that are sewn together along the long edges and then cut apart across the width of the sewn strips to create smaller units.

Template — A pattern used for marking quilt pieces to be cut out.

Triangle-square — In piecing, 2 right triangles joined along their long sides to form a square with a diagonal seam (**Fig. 96**).

Fig. 96

Unit — A pieced section that is made as individual steps in the quilt construction process are completed. Units are usually combined to make blocks or other sections of the quilt top.

CREDITS

We want to extend a warm *thank you* to the generous people who allowed us to photograph our projects at their homes: *A World of Flowers, Crazy About Blue, Lullaby Roses,* and *Romantic Wedding Ring* — Dr. Dan and Sandra Cook; *Garden Wedding and Country Favorite* — Dr. Jerry and Gwen Holton; *Springtime Flower Baskets* — Nancy and Duncan Porter; and *Dresden Plate* — The Hotze House, Little Rock, Arkansas.

The following quilts are from the collection of Bryce and Donna Hamilton, Minneapolis, Minnesota: Double Wedding Ring Quilt, page 8; and Dresden Plate Quilt, page 34.

The Double Wedding Ring Wall Hanging shown on page 11 was created by Katie Mast, Millersburg, Ohio.

Thanks also go to Viking Husqvarna Sewing Machine Company of Cleveland, Ohio, for providing the sewing machines used to make many of the projects in this book.

To Magna IV Color Imaging of Little Rock, Arkansas, we say thank you for the superb color reproduction and excellent pre-press preparation.

We especially want to thank photographers Mark Mathews, Larry Pennington, Karen Busick Shirey, and Ken West of Peerless Photography, Little Rock, Arkansas, and Jerry R. Davis of Jerry Davis Photography, Little Rock, Arkansas, for their time, patience, and excellent work.

We extend a sincere *thank you* to all the people who assisted in making and testing the projects in this book: Karen Call, Debbie Chance, Valerie Doiel, Cheryl Farmer, Wanda Fite, Patricia Galas, Judith H. Hassed, Judith M. Kline, Barbara Middleton, Gazelle Mode, Sherri Mode, Ruby Solida, Glenda Taylor, and Dee Ann Younger; the members of the First Assembly of God Church Women's Ministry, Searcy, Arkansas: Frances Blackburn, Louella English, Wanda Fite, Nan Goode, Bonnie Gowan, Juanita Hodges, Minnie Hogan, Ida Johnson, Ruby Johnson, Richadeen Lewis, Velrie Louks, Della Walters, and Minnie Whitehurst; and members of the Gardner Memorial United Methodist Church Quilters, North Little Rock, Arkansas: Elois Allain, Phula Barnett, Maxie Bramblett, Grace Brooks, Ruth Chronister, Leon Dickey, Alice Dong, Vina Lendermon, Fredda McBride, Edna Sikes, Betty Smith, Esther Starkey, and Thelma Starkey.